In brief

ONS statistical work priorities for 2007–12

On 27 March 2007, the Office for National Statistics (ONS) published a news release entitled 'ONS sets out statistical work priorities for the coming year'.

The key priorities are:

- further investment in improving the population and migration estimates and in preparation for the 2011 Census
- continued investment in modernising ONS systems, including the National Accounts
- a statistical data collection, development and analysis programme which places greater emphasis on the service sector, productivity, and regional policy needs
- a programme of analysis which addresses the priorities of children, ageing and societal welfare
- intensified work on the measurement of public service output and productivity

To accommodate these priorities, ONS will be making a number of changes to current statistical activities as well as proceeding with its efficiency programme. These include:

- optimisation and re-balancing of some of the samples underpinning ONS business surveys
- some reductions in sample sizes for business and household surveys
- reduced detail and changes in frequency for a small number of outputs
- more focused data validation for ONS main business surveys
- reducing the scope of the National Income and Expenditure Blue Book in 2007 to re-allocate resources to modernising the National Accounts

Further information on all of the above can be found in *Plans for the ONS Statistical Work Programme 2007–08* on the National Statistics website, details of which are given below.

ONS, in a further news release published on 15 June, launched a six-week initial consultation programme inviting views on how official statistics should be developed over the next five years. The Office's priorities would then be included in its Statistical Work Programme for 2008–12.

The 2008–12 Statistical Work Programme will be reviewed by the new Statistics Board which is expected to be in place by April 2008, subject to the passage of the Statistics and Registration Services Bill.

More information

www.statistics.gov.uk/statbase/product.asp?vlnk=14823
www.statistics.gov.uk/about/consultations/ons-stat-work-prog.asp

Contact

Glen Watson
01633 812370
glen.watson@ons.gsi.gov.uk

New economic activity interactive pyramids on the National Statistics website

ONS has developed a new and innovative method of showing population data on a dynamic population pyramid. This enables users to see the changes in the structure of the UK population by single years of age through the years. Further development of this method has meant a new version of this pyramid has been developed which shows the composition of the UK in terms of economic activity. Users are now able to view the relative changes in the numbers in employment, numbers unemployed and numbers of economically inactive people through clicking one, two or three boxes on the pyramid. In addition, when the mouse is moved over the pyramid, a table appears on the right hand side which shows figures on the total population (from the Labour Force Survey), the totals and rates in employment, totals and rates of those unemployed and totals and rates of the economically inactive group.

In 2005, the total household population (made up of people who are in employment, unemployed and economically inactive) according to the Labour Force Survey was 47 million. In 1992 this figure was 45 million. This small change in the total number of males and females in the UK hides the dramatic changes which have occurred in the structure of the working age population. Overall, the shape of the working age section of the pyramid (men and women aged between 16 and 64/59, respectively) has altered from being bottom-heavy in 1992, with larger numbers of people in their late 20s and early 30s, to a much more uniform shape in 2005 as these people move up the pyramid. The pyramid enables users to visualise some of the population effects which are able to explain some of the changes seen in employment, unemployment and inactivity rates over the last decade or so. The changes in employment trends over the period can be seen in more detail by using the table of rates. This shows that employment rates for men aged 25 increased from 80 per cent in 1992 to 83 per cent in 2005 but, more strikingly, employment rates for women aged 25 increased from 67 per cent to 76 per cent over the same period. Reflecting these increases in employment, inactivity rates for women aged 25 have declined from 26 per cent in 1992 to 20 per cent in 2005.

To see these and other trends in economic activity since 1992, view the interactive pyramid using the link below. The data shown in the pyramid can be downloaded using links from the pyramid.

More information

www.statistics.gov.uk/economicactivity/index.html

Contact

Catherine Barham
020 7533 5092
catherine.barham@ons.gsi.gov.uk

Introduction of SIC 2007

This major revision of the UK Standard Industrial Classification of Economic Activities (SIC) is the outcome of Operation 2007 – a series of consultations started in 2002 and carried out in conjunction with the major revision of the European Union's industrial classification system, NACE. The consultations involved several stakeholders:

- in the EU, the National Statistical Institutes of all member states and the European Commission
- in the UK, a range of government departments, the Bank of England, the devolved administrations, business and trade associations and other interested bodies

The UK is required by European legislation to revise the SIC in parallel with NACE so that both systems remain identical down to and including the four-digit (class) level. A further breakdown is provided for certain classes by the inclusion of a five-digit (subclass) level. Both the UK SIC and NACE are completely consistent with the UN's International Standard Industrial Classification of all Economic Activities (ISIC), which has itself just been revised.

These revisions are motivated by the need to adapt the classifications to changes in the world economy. The revised classifications reflect the growing importance of service activities in the economies over the last 15 years, mainly due to the developments in information and communication technology (ICT).

Work is under way on the preparation of an introduction and guidance notes to the new classification, correspondence tables between SIC 2003 and SIC 2007, and indexes. These will be published later in 2007.

SIC 2007 will be introduced on the business register and in most annual statistics from the start of 2008. Short-term statistics and National Accounts will move to the new classification later, in accordance with EU requirements. ONS is currently working on an implementation plan for the introduction of the new classification, covering all of its surveys and outputs, and intends publishing this later in the year.

If you are dependent on the SIC in order to produce statistics, or if you are a user of ONS statistics by industry, you need to begin preparing now for the introduction of the new industrial classification! If you would like to know more about the new SIC, or would like help or advice about its introduction, please see the details below. The main document from the first link includes a useful summary table at the front, cross-referencing SIC 2003 and SIC 2007.

More information

www.statistics.gov.uk/statbase/product.
asp?vlnk=14012
www.circa.europa.eu/irc/dsis/nacecpacon/
info/data/en/index.htm

Contact

Mark Williams
 01633 819023
mark.williams@ons.gsi.gov.uk

Joint UNECE/ILO/Eurostat seminar on quality of work

A joint UNECE/ILO/Eurostat seminar on the quality of work was held in Geneva on 18–20 April 2007. Quality of work as a topic was given priority by the last International Conference of

Labour Statisticians, and a task force was set up to develop proposals for indicators that might be used as a measure. The task force presented a framework (with 11 dimensions) to this seminar and some initial indicators that they thought would be largely available, at least in developed countries. The dimensions of the proposed framework were:

- employment opportunities
- unacceptable work
- adequate earnings, skills development and productive work
- asocial/unacceptable hours of work
- stability and security of work
- balancing work and family life
- fair treatment in employment
- safe work
- social protection
- social dialogue and workplace relations, and
- socio-economic context

Some amendments were proposed by the delegates to the seminar and the task force will develop their thoughts further and report progress next year.

The seminar also discussed further papers from potential users of the statistics, including the European Foundation for the Improvement of Living and Working Conditions. A series of case studies from individual countries were also presented, including a paper from ONS on indicators to measure the social dialogue dimensions in the UK.

Details of all the papers for the meeting can be found at the address below.

More information

www.unece.org/stats/documents/2007.04.
labour.htm

Contact

Graeme Walker
 01633 655824
graeme.walker@ons.gsi.gov.uk

Comparisons of statistics on jobs

The coherence and comparability of employment and jobs statistics from different sources is a key quality issue which is of concern to many users of labour market statistics. Ideally there would be a single series of estimates of employment and jobs which are fully consistent, which would be suitable for all purposes.

The Labour Force Survey (LFS), which collects information mainly from residents of private households, is the

main source of statistics on employment (by adding estimates of people with second jobs, corresponding estimates of the number of jobs can be derived). However, the workforce jobs (WFJ) series, which is compiled mainly from surveys of businesses, is the preferred source of statistics on jobs by industry, since it provides a more reliable industry breakdown than the LFS does.

In response to the National Statistics Quality Review of Employment and Jobs Statistics, ONS now regularly publishes comparisons of estimates of jobs from the WFJ series with corresponding estimates from the LFS. Occasional articles are also produced. The latest of these comparisons, currently for the first quarter (March) of 2007, is published as part of the monthly Labour Market Overview, which appears on the National Statistics website at the same time as the Labour Market Statistics First Release. The comparison is updated each quarter, with approximate adjustments made to try to reconcile the main differences between the respective sources. Improvements to these various adjustments are incorporated whenever new information becomes available.

In addition to the recommendations of the Review of Employment and Jobs Statistics, some further recommendations concerning the reconciliation of jobs statistics were made earlier this year by the Workforce Jobs Benchmarking Review, for which an action plan has now also been published. This review highlighted, for example, the issues of coverage of temporary foreign workers, many of whom may, for various reasons, be excluded from LFS data but included in the business surveys used for the WFJ series. Work is proceeding to try to improve these estimates later this year. A review of the method of estimation of the numbers who are self-employed was also identified as a priority. Investigation of data from a new LFS question, introduced this year, on arrangements for paying tax and National Insurance contributions, is now in progress and, subject to the necessary quality assurance, it is hoped this will in due course lead to improvement of the statistics available.

More information

www.statistics.gov.uk/statbase/product.
asp?vlnk=14358
www.statistics.gov.uk/statbase/product.
asp?vlnk=9765

Contact

Andrew Machin
 020 7533 6178
andrew.machin@ons.gsi.gov.uk

national
STATISTICS

Economic & Labour Market Review

July 2007 | Volume 1 | Number 7

Contents

palgrave
macmillan

ISBN 978-0-230-52577-1

ISSN (online) 1751-8334

ISSN (print) 1751-8326

National Statistics are produced to the professional standards set out in the National Statistics Code of Practice. They are produced free from political influence. Not all of the statistics reported on in this publication are within the scope of National Statistics.

The inclusion of reports on studies by non-governmental bodies does not imply endorsement by the Office for National Statistics or any other government department of the views or opinions expressed, nor of the methodology used.

About the Office for National Statistics

The Office for National Statistics (ONS) is the government agency responsible for compiling, analysing and disseminating economic, social and demographic statistics about the UK. It also administers the statutory registration of births, marriages and deaths in England and Wales.

The Director of ONS is also the National Statistician and the Registrar General for England and Wales.

Subscriptions

Annual subscription £200
Single issue £35
To subscribe, contact Palgrave Macmillan at
www.palgrave.com/ons or
  01256 357893

This issue is now available at
www.palgrave-journals.com/elmr and at
www.statistics.gov.uk/elmr

Editorial office

For enquiries about this publication, contact
the Editor, David Harper, *Economic & Labour
Market Review*, Room D4/18, Office for National
Statistics, 1 Drummond Gate, London SW1V 2QQ.
  020 7533 5914
  elmr@ons.gsi.gov.uk

Statistical enquiries

For general enquiries, contact the National
Statistics Customer Contact Centre.
 0845 601 3034
  (minicom: 01633 812399)
  info@statistics.gsi.gov.uk
Post: Room 1015, Government Buildings,
Cardiff Road, Newport, South Wales, NP10 8XG.

You can also find National Statistics on the Internet
at: www.statistics.gov.uk

A fuller list of contact points can be found on
page 68.

UPDATES

Updates to statistics on www.statistics.gov.uk

8 June

Index of production

Manufacturing: 0.4% three-monthly fall to April

www.statistics.gov.uk/cci/nugget. asp?id=198

11 June

Producer prices

Factory gate inflation unchanged at 2.5% in May

www.statistics.gov.uk/cci/nugget.asp?id=248

12 June

Inflation

May: CPI down to 2.5%; RPI at 4.3%

www.statistics.gov.uk/cci/nugget.asp?id=19

UK trade

Deficit narrowed to £3.6 billion in April 2007

www.statistics.gov.uk/cci/nugget.asp?id=199

13 June

Average earnings

Underlying pay growth steady for April 2007

www.statistics.gov.uk/cci/nugget.asp?id=10

Employment

Rate falls to 74.3% in three months to April 2007

www.statistics.gov.uk/cci/nugget.asp?id=12

Public sector

Employment falls in Q1 2007

www.statistics.gov.uk/cci/nugget.asp?id=407

14 June

Retail sales

Firm growth continues

www.statistics.gov.uk/cci/nugget.asp?id=256

20 June

Public sector

May: £6.9 billion current budget deficit

www.statistics.gov.uk/cci/nugget.asp?id=206

21 June

Motor vehicles

Car production rises in the three months to May

www.statistics.gov.uk/cci/nugget.asp?id=376

28 June

Investment

Institutional net investment £13.1 billion in Q1 2007

www.statistics.gov.uk/cci/nugget.asp?id=396

29 June

Balance of payments

2007 Q1: UK deficit falls

www.statistics.gov.uk/cci/nugget.asp?id=194

Business investment

0.6% fall in Q1 2007

www.statistics.gov.uk/cci/nugget.asp?id=258

GDP growth

Economy rose by 0.7% in Q1 2007

www.statistics.gov.uk/cci/nugget.asp?id=192

2 July

Index of services

1.0% three-monthly rise into April

www.statistics.gov.uk/cci/nugget.asp?id=558

Productivity

Productivity growth increases in Q1 2007

www.statistics.gov.uk/cci/nugget.asp?id=133

3 July

Corporate profitability

15.1% in Q1 2007

www.statistics.gov.uk/cci/nugget.asp?id=196

FORTHCOMING RELEASES

Future statistical releases on www.statistics.gov.uk

6 July

Index of production – May 2007

9 July

MQ5: investment by insurance companies, pension funds and trusts – Q1 2007

Producer prices – June 2007

10 July

UK trade – May 2007

11 July

MM19: Aerospace and electronic cost indices – April 2007

13 July

MM24: Monthly review of external trade statistics – May 2007

Share ownership – a report on ownership of shares as at 31 December 2006

16 July

Digest of engineering turnover and orders – May 2007

The ONS Productivity Handbook

17 July

Consumer price indices – June 2007

MM22: Producer prices – June 2007

18 July

Labour market statistics – July 2007

19 July

Public and private sector breakdown of labour disputes

Public sector finances – June 2007

Retail sales – June 2007

SDM28: Retail sales – June 2007

20 July

Gross domestic product (GDP) preliminary estimate – Q2 2007

Index of services – May 2007

The Blue Book – 2007

The Pink Book – 2007

23 July

Focus on consumer price indices – June 2007

24 July

Public sector finances: supplementary (quarterly) data

25 July

Average weekly earnings – May 2007

Motor vehicle production – June 2007

27 July

Distributive and service trades – May 2007

Monthly digest of statistics – July 2007

31 July

Annual Business Inquiry: provisional regional results 2005

3 August

PM 34.10: Motor vehicle production business monitor – June 2007

Economic review

July 2007

Anis Chowdhury
Office for National Statistics

SUMMARY

GDP continued to grow robustly in 2007 quarter one, driven mainly by the services sector, with little contribution from manufacturing output. On the expenditure side, business investment and household spending weakened. As a reflection of the UK's dynamic domestic demand profile and unfavourable exchange rate position, the trade deficit widened through the quarter. The current account deficit narrowed in 2007 quarter one. The labour market remains buoyant despite showing tentative signs of weakening; average earnings remain subdued. The public sector finances deteriorated in May 2007. Consumer price inflation fell and Producer price output inflation was unchanged in May 2007.

GROSS DOMESTIC PRODUCT

First quarter growth of 0.7 per cent

GDP growth for the first quarter of 2007 is estimated to have grown fairly strongly, by 0.7 per cent, unchanged from the initial estimate, but down from the 0.8 per cent growth rate in the previous quarter. The annual rate of growth rose by 3.0 per cent, also down from 3.1 per cent growth in the previous quarter (**Figure 1**).

The growth rate in the UK economy in 2007 quarter one continues to be led by strong growth in services sector output. Total industrial production growth was negative although a slight improvement from the previous quarter, due to a bounce back in mining and quarrying and energy supply output. This was offset by a weakening in manufacturing output. Construction output sustained the strong rate of growth from the previous quarter.

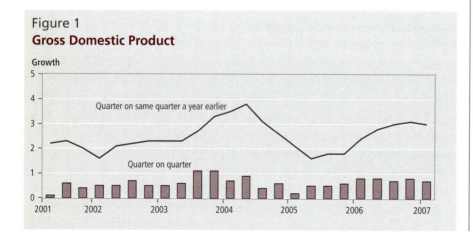

Figure 1
Gross Domestic Product

OTHER MAJOR ECONOMIES

Global growth moderates

Data for 2007 quarter one are now available for the other major OECD countries and these show a slowing picture of the world economy. US GDP data for the first quarter of 2007 showed a weakening. Growth was a subdued 0.2 per cent compared to 0.6 per cent in 2006 quarter four. The lower rate of growth was mainly due a decline in residential investment, continuing the trend from the previous quarter and in line with the weak housing market. The slowdown was also led by a lesser extent due to a weak net export picture with exports falling and imports rising. This was partially offset by a continued robustness in household consumption expenditure, which was underpinned by a fairly buoyant labour market together with a fall in energy prices. Government spending growth also made a positive contribution to GDP growth. Japan's GDP growth also moderated. GDP growth in 2007 quarter one was 0.8 per cent, down from 1.3 per cent in the previous quarter. The slowdown was mainly due to a contraction in private and non-private residential investment as well as business investment. This was partially offset by buoyant household consumption expenditure and partly due to a positive net trade picture with exports rising strongly on the quarter and exceeding imports.

Growth in the three biggest mainland EU economies – Germany, France and Italy – also exhibited signs of weakening. According to Eurostat, euro area GDP grew by 0.6 per cent in 2007 quarter one. This is a deceleration compared to growth of 0.9 per cent growth in the previous quarter. German GDP growth according to the initial estimate was a modest 0.5 percent. This follows fairly strong growth of 1.0 per cent in 2006 quarter four. A weaker net trade position together with a slowdown in household spending contributed towards the modest GDP growth. This was offset by fairly strong growth in industrial output and investment growth. French GDP growth also grew moderately, at 0.5 per cent, similar to the rate in the previous quarter. This reflected a slowdown in manufacturing investment together with household consumption. This was offset by a pick up in household investment and a stronger net trade position. The Italian economy showed a marked deceleration in growth. GDP growth according to the preliminary estimate was just 0.3 per cent in 2007 quarter one, compared to growth of 1.1 per cent in the previous quarter. Early indications suggest that this may mainly have been driven by a fall in industrial production.

FINANCIAL MARKETS

Share prices rise and pound appreciates

Equity performance showed a strong bounce-back in 2007 quarter one, following a weak performance in 2006 quarter four. The FTSE All-Share index rose by around 11.0 per cent in 2007 quarter one after falling by 2.0 per cent in 2006 quarter four; this despite some turbulence towards the end of February 2007 where there was a sharp fall in share prices, partly led by rumours of capital gains taxes on shares in China. The rebound in share prices may be due to a number of factors. Firstly, the rise may have been due to recent speculation about merger activity concerning major companies; secondly, business profitability has been relatively high in recent months, which could have induced share purchases and thirdly, share prices may have risen due to the positive outlook on global growth held by investors. In the first two months of the second quarter of 2007, share prices on average grew by around 3.0 per cent: The slower rate of equity growth may mainly be attributed to higher interest rates and its possible impact, in terms of lower GDP growth and reduced company profitability.

As for currency markets, 2007 quarter one saw sterling's average value appreciating and broadly grow in line with 2006 quarter four. The pound appreciated against the dollar by 2.0 per cent in 2007 quarter one, similar to the rate in the previous quarter. Against the euro, sterling's values appreciated by 0.5 per cent compared to growth of 1.0 per cent in the previous quarter. Overall, the quarterly effective exchange rate appreciated by 1.1 per cent in 2007 quarter one, down from 1.3 per cent growth in 2006 quarter four (**Figure 2**). In the first two months of the second quarter of 2007, sterling appreciated on average by 2.0 per cent against the dollar. Against the euro, sterling was flat. Overall, the effective exchange rate appreciated by around 0.2 per cent.

The recent movements in the exchange rate might be linked to a number of factors.

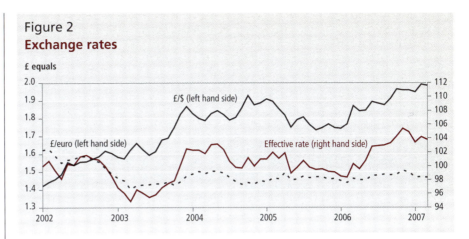

Figure 2
Exchange rates

£ equals

Firstly, exchange rate movements can be related to the perceptions of the relative strengths of the US, the Euro and UK economy. The appreciation of the pound against the both the dollar and euro in 2007 quarter one may be partly linked to perceptions of stronger UK economic growth, leading to greater inflationary pressures and therefore the prospects of higher interest rates in the UK. The potential for future rate rises may have been a factor in sterling's recent appreciation. In fact, interest rates were increased by a further 0.25 percentage point in May 2007, this follows the 0.25 percentage point interest increase in January 2007 and leaves interest rates currently standing at 5.50 per cent.

In contrast, there have been particular concerns in recent months regarding the relative weakness of US GDP growth. Furthermore, inflationary pressures have been relatively subdued in the US. This may have lessened the likelihood of further interest rate rises in the US, which currently stand at 5.25 per cent. In the euro-area, the lower rate of appreciation of the pound against the euro in the first quarter of 2007 may have come in response to further monetary tightening, with the European Central Bank (ECB) raising interest rates by 0.25 percentage points in March 2007. The prospects for future interest rate rises may have weighed as a factor; in fact, interest rates were increased by a further 0.25 percentage points in June to leave interest rates currently standing at 4.0 per cent. The rise in the euro has been further underpinned by relatively robust growth in the euro-zone. However, compared to US and UK rates, euro-zone interest rates still remain fairly moderate and accommodative.

Secondly, another factor for the US depreciation relative to the pound may be due to the current account deficit which is generally seen as a weakness for the

US economy. The dollar may have fallen recently in response to a readjustment process, with the intended consequence of making exports cheaper and imports dearer – thus in theory leading to switch in expenditure to home produced goods and ultimately leading to a narrowing in the deficit.

Thirdly, another factor may be due to a lack of international appetite for dollar denominated assets, particularly from central banks, whom are choosing to mix up their currency assets on their balance sheets (for portfolio and risk management purposes) thereby further undermining the value of the dollar.

OUTPUT

Services sector drives economic growth

GDP growth in 2007 quarter one was estimated at 0.7 per cent, down from 0.8 per cent in the previous quarter. On an annual basis it was 3.0 per cent compared to growth of 3.1 per cent in the previous quarter.

Construction activity is estimated to have grown strongly in the first quarter of 2007. Construction output grew by 0.7 per cent in 2007 quarter one, although a deceleration from growth of 1.1 per cent in the previous quarter. Comparing the quarter on the quarter a year ago, construction output rose by 2.8 per cent following growth of 3.1 per cent in the previous quarter (**Figure 3**).

As for external surveys of construction, the CIPS survey signalled strengthening activity in 2007 quarter one with the average headline index at 58.0, up from 56.8 in the previous quarter. Stronger activity was driven by a rise in commercial activity. In May 2007, the headline index was 58.0. The RICS in its 2007 quarter one construction survey report that growth in construction workloads accelerated further

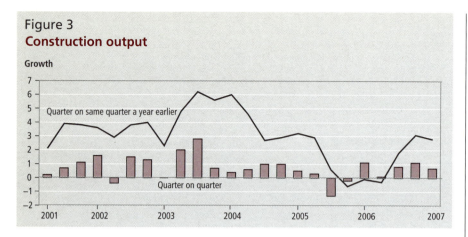

Figure 3
Construction output

in the first quarter of 2007 and at the fastest pace since 2004 quarter two. The net survey balance was at 28 per cent, up from 26 per cent in 2006 quarter four.

Total output from the production industries fell by 0.1 per cent in 2007 quarter one after falling by 0.2 per cent in the previous quarter. On an annual basis it also fell by 0.1 per cent compared to growth of 0.9 per cent in the previous quarter. The main contributions to the pick up in the latest quarter came from a turnaround in mining & quarrying output (including oil & gas production) which rose by 1.0 per cent in 2007 quarter one after decreasing by 1.0 per cent in the previous quarter. This was mainly due to oil extraction from the start up of the Buzzard oil-field. Electricity, gas and water supply output also grew, by 1.5 per cent, reversing a fall of 2.0 per cent in the previous quarter. This mainly reflected the resumption of power from two nuclear power stations. Manufacturing output in contrast fell by 0.4 per cent, a weakening from growth of just 0.1 per cent in the previous quarter. On an annual basis, manufacturing output also weakened but still showed a fairly robust rate of growth. Growth was 1.1 per cent compared to 2.6 per cent in 2006 quarter four (**Figure 4**). Production growth has generally been weak since the second quarter of 2006 due to weakness in mining and quarrying and utilities output, offset through most of this period by relatively strong manufacturing output. In the latest quarter, the picture has somewhat reversed with manufacturing output weakening. This may be due to the appreciation of sterling which makes British goods more expensive to sell overseas; and possibly due to slower US economic growth. The output of the agriculture, forestry and fishing industries rose by 0.8 per cent following flat growth in the previous quarter.

External surveys of manufacturing for 2007 quarter one show a relatively strong

picture (**Figure 5**). It is not unusual for the path of business indicators and official data to diverge over the short term. These differences happen partly because the series are not measuring exactly the same thing. External surveys measure the direction rather than the magnitude of a change in output and often inquire into expectations rather than actual activity.

The CIPS average headline index for manufacturing indicated a strengthening picture in 2007 quarter one. The headline index was 54.4, up from 52.9 in 2006 quarter four, indicative of fairly robust growth. Growth was led by both increases in output and new orders. In May 2007, the headline index edged up further to

57.5. The CBI in its 2007 quarter one Industrial Trends survey reported growth in manufacturers' level of total orders being the strongest than at any time in the last decade, with the balance at plus 2. The latest monthly Industrial Trends survey in June recorded a strengthening, with the orders balance at plus 8. The BCC survey reported a weakening, but overall, still a fairly buoyant picture in 2007 quarter one. The net balance for home sales fell to plus 27 from plus 31 in 2006 quarter four.

Overall the service sector, by far the largest part of the UK economy, continues to be the main driver of UK growth. Growth was 0.9 per cent in 2007 quarter one, down from 1.1 per cent growth in the previous quarter (**Figure 6**). On an annual basis, growth was 3.8 per cent, up from 3.6 per cent in the previous quarter. Growth was recorded across all sectors. The main contribution to the growth rate continues to be driven by business services and finance output which grew by 1.0 per cent in the latest quarter, down marginally from 1.1 per cent in the previous quarter. Transport, storage and communication also grew strongly at 1.6 per cent, similar to the rate in the previous quarter. There was also fairly robust growth in the output of the distribution, hotels and catering sector. Growth was 1.0 per cent compared to

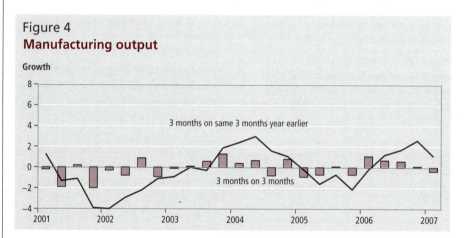

Figure 4
Manufacturing output

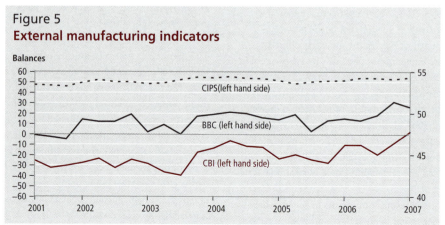

Figure 5
External manufacturing indicators

Figure 6
Services output

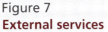

Growth

Quarter on same quarter a year earlier

Quarter on quarter

1.5 per cent in the previous quarter. The output of government and other services grew by a modest 0.5 per cent, down from 0.6 per cent in the previous quarter.

The external surveys on services continued to show a fairly robust picture in line with the official picture. The CIPS average headline index in 2007 quarter one was 58.1, down from 59.9 in the previous quarter and continued to be led by new orders. In May 2007, the index had nudged down to 57.2. It should be noted that the CIPS survey has a narrow coverage of the distribution and government sectors.

The CBI and BCC also report a fairly buoyant picture (**Figure 7**). The CBI in its latest services sector survey in May reported strong growth in business volumes for both consumer and business & professional services firms over the last three months. The consumer services volume balance was at plus 44 and for business & professional services, the balance was at plus 27. The BCC in its 2007 quarter one survey reported a weakening in domestic balances but overall the balances remain relatively strong. The net balance for home sales fell 7 points to plus 27. The net balance for home orders fell 2 points to plus 28 in 2007 quarter one.

The UK sectoral account shows the UK corporate sector once again as being a big net lender in 2007 quarter one. Despite the surplus, the overall debt level remains high due to the heavy borrowing between 1997 and 2001. The household sector remains a net borrower as income growth proved insufficient to finance total outlays. Households debt levels continue be relatively high, although the quarterly interest payments on the loans are still being kept down by low interest rates as a proportion of income, although they have steadily increased in recent quarters due to rises in interest rates. The level of central government borrowing fell in 2007 quarter

one from the previous quarter, but remains high due to higher rises in cash expenditure exceeding tax receipts. The current account of the UK balance of payments continues to be in deficit.

EXPENDITURE

Consumers' spending weakens

Household consumption expenditure growth decelerated in 2007 quarter one. Growth was a fairly modest 0.5 per cent. This follows relatively strong growth of 1.1 per cent in the previous

quarter. Growth compared with the same quarter a year ago was 2.9 per cent, up from 2.5 per cent in the previous quarter (**Figure 8**). In terms of expenditure breakdown, the slowdown was led by virtually flat growth in semi-durable goods expenditure, compared to strong growth in the previous quarter. There was also a weakening in non-durable goods and services expenditure. This was offset by buoyant growth in expenditure on durable goods, although slowing from the previous quarter.

Household expenditure in 2007 quarter one could have weakened for a number of economic reasons. Firstly, one key indicator of household expenditure is retail sales. Retail sales appear to have slowed in 2007 quarter one from the previous quarter. Retail sales grew by 0.4 per cent in the latest quarter, a marked deceleration from growth of 1.4 per cent in the previous quarter. The drop in retail sales occurred despite heavy discounting in the shops with the price deflator (that is, shop prices) falling on average by 0.4 per cent in the latest quarter. This may suggest a change in underlying fundamentals, particularly in regards to household disposable income and/or, it could be interpreted as a sign of caution on

Figure 7
External services

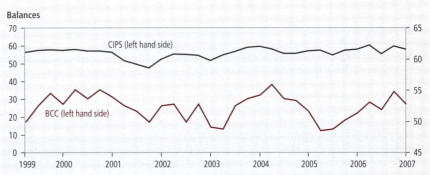

Balances

CIPS (left hand side)

BCC (left hand side)

Figure 8
Household demand

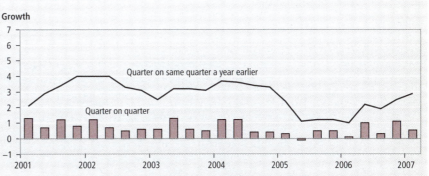

Growth

Quarter on same quarter a year earlier

Quarter on quarter

the part of consumers, wishing to retrench given the strong spending undertaken in the previous quarter.

Retail sales figures are published on a monthly basis and the latest available figures for May showed buoyant growth, roughly similar to the previous month (**Figure 9**). This may suggest that going into the second quarter, interest rate rises don't seem to be having much of an impact on spending as it did in the first quarter and also despite the average rise of the price deflator of around 0.8 per cent in the second quarter. According to the latest figures, the volume of retail sales in the three months to May 2007 was 1.1 per cent higher than the previous three months. This followed growth of 1.2 per cent in the three months to April. On an annual basis, retail sales continued to grow strongly. Retail sales on the latest three month on the same three months a year ago rose by 4.4 per cent, compared to 4.8 per cent in the three months to April compared to the same period a year ago.

At a disaggregated level, retail sales growth during the three months to the end of May was driven by a sharp acceleration in growth in the 'Predominantly non-food stores' sector which grew by 1.5 per cent, down from 1.7 per cent growth in the

previous month. Within this sector in the three months to May, growth was led by the 'Other stores' sector which grew by 3.5 per cent. The 'Textile, clothing and footwear stores' sector also registered strong growth at 2.9 per cent followed by the 'Non-store retailing and repair' sector (which includes mail order and internet sales) where sales grew by 2.2 per cent. In contrast, the 'Household goods stores' sector saw sales volume fall by 1.5 per cent, a weakening from the 0.9 per cent fall in April. Retail sales growth in the 'Predominantly food stores' sector recorded modest growth of 0.4 per cent, the same as in the previous two months.

External surveys for retail show weakening, but overall still a fairly robust picture. The CBI in its monthly Distributive Trades survey report that retail sales volumes slowed for the second successive month to a balance of plus 17 in June from plus 31 in May. The BRC report that retail sales increased by 1.8 per cent on a like-for-like basis in May, down from 2.4 per cent in the previous month (**Figure 10**).

Household consumption has risen faster than disposable income in recent years as the household sector has become a considerable net borrower and therefore accumulated high debt levels. Bank of England data on stocks of household debt

outstanding to banks and building societies shows household debt at unprecedented levels relative to disposable income.

There are two channels of borrowing available to households; i) secured lending, usually on homes; and ii) unsecured lending, for example, on credit cards. On a general level, increases in interest rates increases debt servicing costs and in the process may have displaced consumer expenditure on certain goods.

The financial account shows that the general movement from net lending to borrowing since 1992 has primarily been facilitated by increases in both secured and unsecured lending. In 2007 quarter one there appears to be signs of a slowdown in both. Lending continues to be driven by loans on secured dwellings. However, in the latest quarter, borrowing secured on dwellings fell to around £22 billion from around £30 billion in the previous quarter. Unsecured lending also fell to around £600 million from around £1.1 billion in 2006 quarter four.

The slowdown in household spending may also be a reflection of a fall in real households' disposable income in the latest quarter (**Figure 11**). Real household disposable income weakened further in 2007 quarter with negative growth of 0.3 per cent, up from a 0.1 per cent decrease in the previous quarter. The fall in real households' disposable income could be partly attributable to a rise in taxes as a share of income in 2007 quarter one, which rose by 4.7 per cent on the quarter, reversing a fall of 0.6 per cent in the previous quarter (**Figure 12**).

Another factor for the slowdown could be attributed to house prices, which although still growing fairly buoyantly, are beginning to show an underlying picture of slowdown, suggesting the lagged effect of the three interest rate rises may be starting to feed through to housing demand. According to the Nationwide, house prices grew by 2.0 per cent in 2007 quarter one, down from 2.1 per cent growth in the previous quarter. Halifax report that overall, house prices grew by 2.8 per cent in 2007 quarter one, well below the 4.2 per cent rise in 2006 quarter four. According to the latest figures, Halifax reported annual house price growth of 10.0 per cent in April, down from 10.7 per cent growth in March. Nationwide also report signs of cooling in the housing market. Although the annual rate grew by 10.3 per cent, the underlying trend slowed

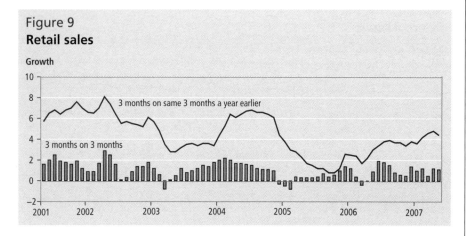

Figure 9
Retail sales

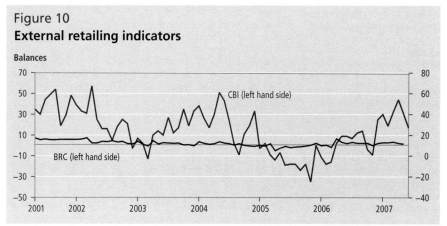

Figure 10
External retailing indicators

Figure 11
Real households' disposable income

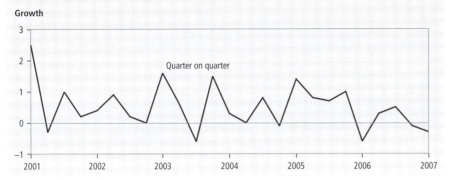

of the pound and its further recent appreciation, particularly against the dollar may, aligned with a slowdown in the US economy have been a factor. The high pound may have made it difficult to sell UK goods to the US which is a major export market. Secondly, high real interest rates may have made investment in financial assets a much more favourable investment proposition than physical assets which may have been reflected in increased share buying and merger activity recently. Thirdly, firms may have been reluctant to investment due to an attempt to build up their profit base.

According to the sectoral accounts, the private non-financial corporate sector was a net lender in 2007 quarter one lending £7.9 billion, up from £5.7 billion in the previous quarter. This is mainly due to reinvested earnings on direct foreign investment. Corporate sector debt levels remain high despite the sector surplus of recent years. The financial balance sheet shows the corporate sector had net liabilities of £1.9 billion.

Evidence on investment intentions from the latest BCC and CBI surveys showed a mixed picture. According to the quarterly BCC survey, the balance of manufacturing firms planning to increase investment in plant and machinery fell 5 points to plus 18 and in services firms rose by 2 points to plus 20 in 2007 quarter one. The CBI in its 2007 quarter one Industrial Survey reported a subdued investment picture, with the investment balance at minus seven.

Figure 12
Taxation as a share of income

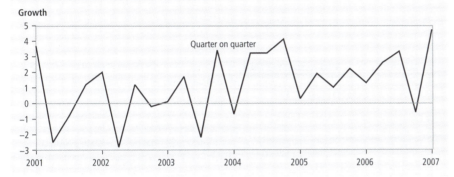

with the three-month on three-month growth rate falling by 1.8 per cent in May; its lowest level since 2006.

The slowdown in house prices may have affected household consumption in a number of ways. Firstly, by reducing the feel-good factor; secondly, lower housing demand may have lead to lower expenditure on household items; thirdly, one source of expenditure has come through equity release, a lower rate of house price growth could have lead to a lower level of borrowing to finance further consumption.

Higher inflation could be another possible factor. Finally, although the labour market appears relatively healthy, wage growth has been weak in real terms recently and this may act to a certain extent as a constraint on expenditure.

Business investment weakens

Total investment slowed down in 2007 quarter one from the previous quarter but continues to show a fairly robust rate of growth. Growth was 1.1 per cent compared to 3.1 per cent in 2006 quarter four. On an annual basis it grew by 8.9 per cent compared to 9.8 per cent in the previous quarter. The weakening in total investment was primarily driven by a contraction in business investment.

Business investment grew relatively strongly throughout 2006. However, in the latest quarter, this previously benign position has somewhat turned around. Business investment in 2007 quarter one fell by 0.6 per cent, reversing the relatively strong growth of 4.1 per cent in the previous quarter. Business investment on an annual basis slowed but still continues to grow fairly robustly. Growth was 9.4 per cent, down from 12.8 per cent annual growth in the previous quarter (**Figure 13**). There could be a number of economic reasons explaining this downturn in business investment. Firstly, the continued strength

Government expenditure showed modest growth

Government final consumption expenditure grew moderately in 2007 quarter one. Growth was 0.5 per cent, similar to the rate in the

Figure 13
Total fixed investment

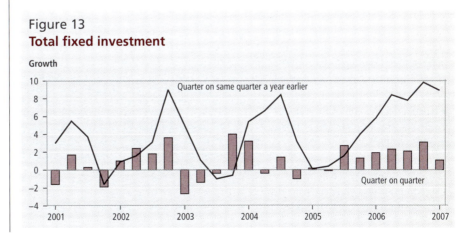

Figure 14
Government spending

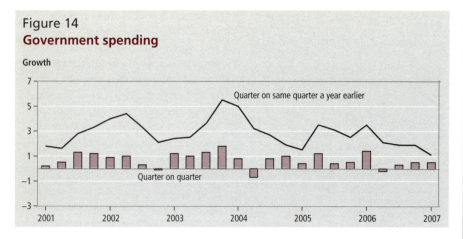

previous quarter. Growth quarter on quarter a year ago was a fairly strong 1.1 per cent, but a deceleration of growth from 1.9 per cent in the previous quarter (**Figure 14**).

Public sector finances worsen

The latest figures on the public sector finances report in the current financial year to May 2007 and illustrated a mixed picture. It showed a higher current budget deficit together with a lower level of net borrowing. Overall however, the government continued to operate a financial deficit, with government expenditure continuing to exceed revenues, partly to fund capital spending. In May 2007, the current budget was in deficit by £6.9 billion; this compares with a deficit of £6.3 billion in May of 2006. In the financial year April to May 2007/08, the deficit was £6.6 billion; this compares with a deficit of £6.3 billion in the financial year April to May 2006. Net borrowing was £8.2 billion in May 2007; this compares with £7.7 billion in May 2006. In the financial year April to May 2007/08, net borrowing was £9.4 billion; this compares with net borrowing of £9.7 billion in the financial year April to May 2006/07. The overall negative picture mainly reflected a sharp fall in corporation and petroleum revenue tax receipts, together with a higher level of central government borrowing.

The financial account shows that the issuance of both sterling treasury bills and government securities has financed this net borrowing. The latest quarter saw the outstanding amount of government securities at £440.0 billion and of Treasury bills at £15.6 billion.

Since net borrowing became positive in 2002, following the current budget moving from surplus into deficit, net debt as a proportion of annual GDP has risen

steadily. Public sector net debt in May 2007 was 37.2 per cent of GDP, up from 36.8 per cent in April. This compares with 36.5 per cent of GDP in May 2006. In the financial year 2006/07, net debt as a percentage of GDP was 37.2 per cent.

TRADE AND THE BALANCE

Current account deficit narrows

The publication of the latest quarterly Balance of Payments shows that the current account deficit narrowed in 2007 quarter one to £12.2 billion, from a deficit of £14.5 billion in the previous quarter (**Figure 15**). As a proportion of GDP, the deficit fell to 3.6 per cent of GDP from 4.3 per cent in 2006 quarter four. The narrowing in current account deficit in 2007 quarter one was due to a higher surplus on investment income and a higher surplus on trade in services, partially offset by a higher deficit in the trade in goods. The surplus in income rose to £3.4 billion from £1.4 billion, while the surplus in the trade in services rose to £8.5 billion from £7.9 billion. The increase in income was driven by a rise in earnings on other investment abroad and on portfolio investment, which outweighed a fall in earnings on direct investment abroad.

The run of current account deficits since 1998 reflects the sustained deterioration in the trade balance. The UK has traditionally run a surplus on the trade in services, complemented by a surplus in investment income, but this has been more than offset by the growing deficit in trade in goods partly due to the UK's appetite for cheaper imports.

Data for 2007 quarter one showed the UK continuing to have a large trade deficit in goods with levels of imports rising faster than exports. This has provided a negative contribution towards GDP growth in the first quarter. The deficit on trade in goods in 2007 quarter one was £20.8 billion, compared with a deficit of £20.0 billion in the previous quarter. In terms of growth, exports of goods fell by 2.5 per cent in 2007 quarter one whilst imports of goods fell by 0.9 per cent. Services exports rose by 2.1 per cent whilst services imports were flat. Total exports fell by 0.8 per cent whilst total imports fell by 0.7 per cent.

The appreciation of the pound recently may have been a factor for the relatively higher trade deficit, as a higher pound makes imports cheaper and exports more expensive.

According to the latest trade figures in April, the UK's deficit on trade in goods and services is estimated at £3.6 billion, down from £4.5 billion in March. Total exports fell by 0.9 per cent and total imports fell by 4.0 per cent on the month. In the three months ended April, the deficit on trade in goods and services was £12.3 billion, unchanged from the previous three months. In terms of growth, total exports fell by 2.3 per cent and total imports fell by 1.2 per cent.

However, these figures are distorted by volatility in VAT Missing Trader Intra–Community (MTIC) Fraud and therefore needs to be treated with caution. According to the latest figures, the level of trade in goods excluding trade associated with

Figure 15
Balance of payments

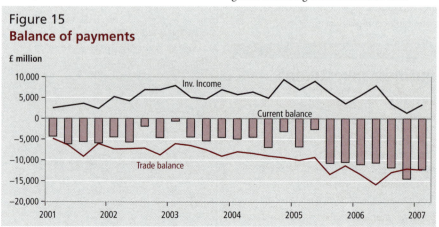

MTIC fraud is estimated to have fallen to £0.1 billion in April and by £0.3 billion in the first quarter of 2007.

Overall, the persistence of the current account deficit has led to the deterioration in the UK's international investment position (IIP) with the rest of the world. The net asset/liability was negative to the tune of £302.8 billion at the end of the first quarter of 2007 compared with net external liabilities of £291.9 billion at the end of the previous quarter. UK assets abroad increased by £455.7 billion from the end of the fourth quarter to a level of £5,738.0 billion at the end of the first quarter. UK liabilities increased by £466.6 billion over the same period to a level of £6,040.8 billion. The rise in the level of both UK assets and UK liabilities in the first quarter reflects both net investment and price movements.

External surveys on exports show a mixed picture. The BCC reported that the export sales net balance rose by 1 point to plus 21 and the export orders balance fell 1 point to plus 20 in 2007 quarter one. The CBI in its 2007 quarter one Industrial Trends Survey reported that both export sales and orders were flat at zero balances. According to the latest CBI monthly Industrial Trends survey, the export balance was at minus 8 in May.

LABOUR MARKET

Labour market activity still fairly buoyant

The Labour market in the latest reference period showed a mixed picture. There appears to be some signs of weakening in the Labour market. This somewhat reverses the recent trend of fairly strong growth in labour market activity; as a result of a feeding through of fairly strong demand conditions from the beginning of 2006 into a strengthened labour market picture. Overall however, the labour market can still be considered as remaining rather buoyant, with employment and unemployment at fairly stable levels compared to the beginning of the year. Taking all the indicators together, the picture remains inconclusive as to suggest the labour market was entering a looser period.

The latest figure from the Labour Force Survey (LFS) pertains to the three-month period up to April 2007 and mostly showed a mixed picture. The number

Figure 16
Employment and unemployment

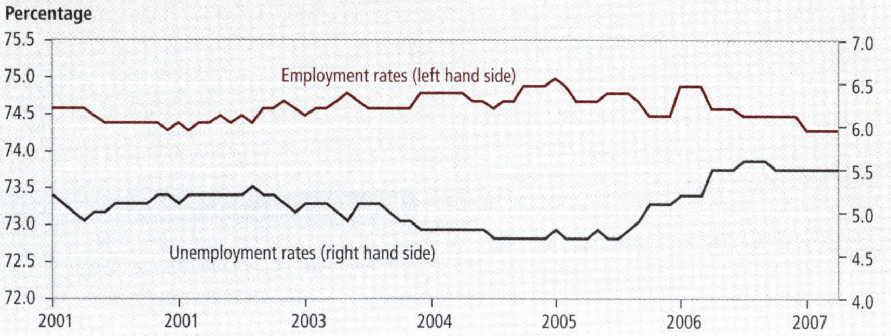

of people in employment fell as did the employment rate. On the upside, the number of unemployed people and the claimant count fell. The unemployment rate was unchanged. Job vacancies increased. Average earnings, excluding bonuses was unchanged, while average earnings including bonuses fell; but overall, average earnings remain subdued with weak real wage growth.

Looking at a detailed level, the fall in the employment level appears to be mainly driven by a fall in employees, particularly part time employees, offset by an increase in the number of people in self-employment, continuing the trend of the recent months.

The current working age employment rate was 74.3 per cent, in the three months to April 2007, down 0.1 percentage points from the three months to January 2007 and down 0.3 percentage points from a year earlier. The number of people in employment fell by 10,000 over the quarter, but was up 87,000 over the year, to leave the employment level standing at 29.01 million in the three months to April 2007. The unemployment rate was 5.5 per cent, in the three months to April 2007, unchanged from the three months to January 2007 and up 0.2 percentage points from a year earlier (**Figure 16**). The number of unemployed people fell by 15,000, from the three months to January, but was up 58,000 from a year earlier, leaving the unemployment level currently standing at 1.68 million.

According to the LFS, in the period February to April 2007, the number of people in employment fell by 10,000. The decrease was led by a fall in employees of 19,000 offset by an increase in self-employment of 6,000. From another perspective, the number of people in full-time employment rose by 31,000, whilst people in part-time employment fell by 42,000.

Workforce jobs falls

According to employer surveys, there was a decrease of 22,000 jobs in the three months to March 2007. Most sectors showed decreases in jobs over the quarter. The largest quarterly contribution came from falls in agriculture, forestry & fishing (down 22,000), followed by transport & communication (down 21,000) and manufacturing (down 16,000). This was offset by increases in finance and business services (up 32,000) followed by distribution hotels & restaurants (up 11,000). Over the year, total workforce jobs increased by 265,000. Of the total, the largest contribution to the increase came from finance and business services (up 126,000) followed by construction (up 75,000) and education, health and public administration (up 63,000). The manufacturing sector in contrast lost the largest number of jobs on the year (down 43,000 jobs), followed by transport and communication (down 24,000).

Claimant count falls

The claimant count measures the number of people claiming the Jobseekers Allowance. The latest figures for May showed the claimant count level at 880,400, down 9,300 on the month and down 71,500 on a year earlier. The claimant count rate in May 2007 was 2.7 per cent, virtually unchanged from the previous month and down 0.2 percentage points from a year earlier.

Vacancies rise

The number of vacancies created in the UK continued to show a healthy demand position for the economy, and appears to belie the weakness of the labour market in respect to the employment indicators. It may simply be the case that there is a mismatch between skills and vacancies and/or it could be an indication of the time lag in filling vacancies. There were 638, 800 job vacancies on average in the three months to May 2007, up 21, 700 from the previous three months and up 54, 400 from the same period a year earlier.

Inactivity level rises

The working age inactivity rate was 21.3 per cent in the three months to April 2007, up 0.2 percentage points from the three months to January 2007 and from a year earlier. In level terms, the number of economically inactive people of working age was up 77,000 over the quarter to leave the level standing at 7.95 million in the three months to April 2007. There were inactivity increases amongst most categories over the quarter. The largest increase in inactivity level occurred amongst those categorised as 'student' (up 30,000), followed by those categorised as 'looking after family/home' (up 29,000) and the 'long-term sick' category (up 14,000). On an annual basis, inactivity rose by 120,000, with the largest rises being amongst those categorised as 'student' (up 36,000), followed by the 'retired' category (up 23,000) and 'temporary sick' (up 16,000).

Average earnings remain subdued

Average earnings growth showed a mixed picture in April 2007, but the underlying picture is still that of relative weakness. Average earnings (including bonuses) decreased in the latest reference period. It fell by 0.4 percentage points from the previous month to 4.0 per cent. Average earnings growth (excluding bonuses) was 3.6 per cent, unchanged from the previous month. In terms of the public and private sector split, the gap in wages narrowed slightly. Average earnings (excluding bonuses) grew by 3.1 in the public sector, up 0.1 percentage point from the previous month, and grew by 3.7 per cent in the private sector, down 0.1 percentage points from the previous month.

Despite the weakening in labour market activity in the latest period, overall, the numbers still point to a fairly buoyant labour market, although it is still

loose compared to previous years, with employment levels at relatively high levels and unemployment at a fairly stable level. This is consistent with higher workforce participation rates, underpinned by robust GDP growth. Average earnings show stable but fairly modest growth, consistent with increased supply in the labour force.

PRICES

Producer output prices unchanged; producer input prices rise

Industrial input and output prices are an indication of inflationary pressures in the economy. In 2007 quarter one, output prices exhibited signs of further acceleration of growth from 2006 quarter four and therefore signs of greater inflationary pressures. However, input prices fell on average in the first quarter of 2007 in contrast to an increase in the previous quarter. This may suggest that firms to some extent have attempted to rebuild their profit margins by passing on the higher price of their products to customers, after facing profit squeeze of previous quarters.

Input prices on average fell by 0.9 per cent in 2007 quarter one, on the back of lower oil prices. This contrasts with 2006 quarter four where prices on average increased by 3.5 per cent. The core input price index, excluding food, beverages, tobacco and petroleum rose by 1.7 per cent in 2007 quarter one compared to growth of 4.9 per cent in 2006 quarter four. The slower growth in input prices was to some extent helped by the appreciation of the pound relative to the dollar and euro, which had the effect of making exports dearer but imports cheaper. According to the latest figures, input prices rose by 1.2 per cent in the year to May 2007, reversing the decrease of 0.8 per cent

in April. The main contribution to the rise in the twelve months to May came from higher metal prices which rose by 16.5 per cent, partially offset by lower gas and crude petroleum prices of 27.5 per cent and 0.2 per cent respectively. In May, core input prices rose sharply, by 3.3 per cent compared to 1.8 per cent in April.

Output prices grew on average by 2.4 per cent in 2007 quarter one, a significant strengthening from growth of 1.9 per cent in the previous quarter, and as mentioned earlier may be an attempt by firms to re-build their profit margins. The underlying picture also suggested greater inflationary pressures. On the core measure which excludes food, beverages, tobacco and petroleum, producer output prices rose by 2.7 per cent in 2007 quarter one, up from 2.5 per cent in the previous quarter. According to the latest figures, the growth of the output price index was 2.5 per cent in the year to May, unchanged from the previous month but still indicative of inflationary pressures. However, it may also suggest firms' unwillingness to pass on higher costs despite the rise in input prices in May. The main contribution to the rise in output prices came from the 'Other product' group where prices rose by 4.4 per cent followed by the 'Tobacco & alcohol' group and 'Metal products' group, each growing by 4.3 per cent respectively. On the core measure, output prices also showed stable growth. The core output price index rose by 2.4 per cent in the year to May, unchanged from April.

Consumer prices fall

Growth in the consumer price index (CPI) – the Government's target measure of inflation – fell in May to 2.5 per cent from 2.8 per cent in April and

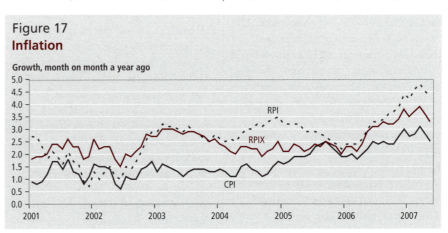

Figure 17
Inflation

Growth, month on month a year ago

from the March peak of 3.1 per cent; but still continuing to exceed the Government's 2.0 per cent inflation target. The Retail Price Index (RPI) a broader measure of inflation also fell, to 4.3 per from 4.5 per cent in April. The Retail Price Index, excluding mortgage interest payments (RPIX) was 3.3 per cent, down from 3.6 per cent in April (**Figure 17**).

The main downward pressure on the CPI annual rate came from average gas and electricity bills which continued to fall this year, but rose a year ago. There was also downward pressure from food and non-alcoholic beverages, mainly due to vegetable prices falling this year, reflecting good supplies following favourable growing conditions and reports of low demand for some produce. By contrast, vegetable prices rose last year. There was also a large downward effect from changes in the price of meat.

A further large downward effect came from clothing and footwear, where prices were little changed this year but rose a year ago for outerwear, with the main downward contributions coming from jeans and women's skirts. Small downward effects also came from underwear and clothing accessories.

The main upward pressure on the CPI annual rate came from transport, with large price increases in the cost of air travel, particularly for transatlantic and European routes. Last year, by contrast, fares fell in May, having risen sharply in April when the price collection period coincided with Easter. This year, Easter fell earlier in the month.

RPI inflation was influenced by similar factors to those that affected the CPI. Mortgage interest payments, which are excluded from the CPI, had a small upward contribution to the change in the RPI annual rate, with some lenders passing on this May's quarter point increase in the Bank Rate.

Key indicators

The data in this table support the Economic review by providing some of the latest estimates of Key indicators.

Seasonally adjusted unless otherwise stated

	Source CDID	2005	2006	2006 Q3	2006 Q4	2007 Q1	2007 Mar	2007 Apr	2007 May
GDP growth - chained volume measures (CVM)									
Gross domestic product at market prices	ABMI	1.8	2.8	0.7	0.8	0.7	..	..	..
Output growth – chained volume measures (CVM)									
Gross value added (GVA) at basic prices	ABMM	1.9	2.9	0.7	0.8	0.7	..	..	..
Industrial production	CKYW	−2.0	0.0	0.1	−0.1	−0.1	0.1	0.3	..
Manufacturing	CKYY	−1.2	1.3	0.6	0.1	−0.4	0.5	0.3	..
Construction	GDQB	1.5	1.0	0.8	1.1	0.6	..	..	..
Services	GDQS	2.9	3.6	0.8	1.0	1.0	..	..	..
Oil and gas extraction	CKZO	−10.5	−8.9	−3.1	−1.1	0.7	−2.8	1.0	..
Electricity, gas and water supply	CKYZ	−0.4	−2.6	−0.1	−2.0	1.5	−0.9	−0.8	..
Business services and finance	GDQN	4.4	5.2	1.3	1.0	1.0	..	..	..
Household demand									
Retail sales volume growth	EAPS	2.0	3.3	0.8	1.4	0.5	0.5	−0.1	0.4
Household final consumption expenditure growth (CVM)	ABJR	1.5	1.9	0.3	1.1	0.5	..	..	..
GB new registrations of cars (thousands)1	BCGT	2,444	2,340	662	446	678	445	168	..
Labour market[2,3]									
Employment: 16 and over (thousands)	MGRZ	28,674	28,895	28,986	29,036	28,981	29,012	..	..
Employment rate: working age (%)	MGSU	74.7	74.6	74.5	74.5	74.3	74.3	..	..
Workforce jobs (thousands)	DYDC	31,042	31,409	31,494	31,608	31,587	..	..	..
Total actual weekly hours of work: all workers (millions)	YBUS	918.6	923.7	925.4	925.8	927.1	925.9	..	..
Unemployment: 16 and over (thousands)	MGSC	1,426	1,657	1,711	1,687	1,700	1,677	..	..
Unemployment rate: 16 and over (%)	MGSX	4.7	5.4	5.6	5.5	5.5	5.5	..	..
Claimant count (thousands)	BCJD	861.7	944.7	955.0	947.1	916.3	905.7	889.7	880.4
Economically active: 16 and over (thousands)	MGSF	30,100	30,552	30,696	30,723	30,681	30,689	..	..
Economic activity rate: working age (%)	MGSO	78.5	78.9	79.0	79.0	78.8	78.7	..	..
Economically inactive: working age (thousands)	YBSN	7,933	7,843	7,835	7,854	7,939	7,954	..	..
Economic inactivity rate: working age (%)	YBTL	21.5	21.1	21.0	21.0	21.2	21.3	..	..
Vacancies (thousands)	AP2Y	616.8	594.9	598.9	602.0	635.1	635.1	637.1	638.8
Redundancies (thousands)	BEAO	126	145	141	130	145	129	..	..
Productivity and earnings annual growth									
GB average earnings (including bonuses)[3]	LNNC	..	..	3.9	4.0	4.4	4.4	4.0	..
GB average earnings (excluding bonuses)[3]	JQDY	..	..	3.5	3.7	3.6	3.6	3.6	..
Whole economy productivity (output per worker)	A4YN	..	..	2.4	2.1	2.7	..	..	..
Manufacturing productivity (output per job)	LOUV	..	..	..	..	..	3.6	3.5	..
Unit wage costs: whole economy	LOJE	..	..	1.9	1.6	2.4	..	..	..
Unit wage costs: manufacturing	LOJF	..	..	..	..	..	−0.1	−0.2	..
Business demand									
Business investment growth (CVM)	NPEL	15.7	−4.2	3.0	4.1	−0.6	..	..	..
Government demand									
Government final consumption expenditure growth	NMRY	2.7	2.4	0.3	0.5	0.5	..	..	..
Prices (12–monthly percentage change – except oil prices)									
Consumer prices index[1]	D7G7	2.1	2.3	2.4	2.7	2.9	3.1	2.8	2.5
Retail prices index[1]	CZBH	2.8	3.2	3.5	4.0	4.5	4.8	4.5	4.3
Retail prices index (excluding mortgage interest payments)	CDKQ	2.3	2.9	3.2	3.5	3.7	3.9	3.6	3.3
Producer output prices (excluding FBTP)4	EUAA	2.1	2.3	2.3	2.6	2.6	2.7	2.4	2.3
Producer input prices	EUAB	11.7	9.5	7.9	3.4	−0.7	0.7	−0.7	1.1
Oil price: sterling (£ per barrel)	ETXR	30.358	35.929	37.748	31.637	29.946	32.065	34.019	32.639
Oil price: dollars ($ per barrel)	ETXQ	55.046	66.107	70.675	60.633	58.527	62.455	67.646	64.760

	Source CDID	2005	2006	2006 Q3	2006 Q4	2007 Q1	2007 Mar	2007 Apr	2007 May
Financial markets									
Sterling ERI (January 2005=100)	BK67	100.5	101.0	102.2	103.5	104.6	103.4	104.2	103.8
Average exchange rate /US$	AUSS	1.820	1.843	1.875	1.917	1.955	1.947	1.991	1.984
Average exchange rate /Euro	THAP	1.463	1.467	1.471	1.485	1.492	1.470	1.471	1.468
3–month inter–bank rate	HSAJ	4.57	5.26	5.02	5.26	5.56	5.56	5.66	5.76
Selected retail banks: base rate	ZCMG						5.25	5.25	5.50
3–month interest rate on US Treasury bills	LUST	3.92	4.89	4.77	4.89	4.91	4.91	4.79	4.71
Trade and the balance of payments									
UK balance on trade in goods (£m)	BOKI	−68,789	−83,631	−19,907	−20,040	−20,818	−7,157	−6,316	..
Exports of services (£m)	IKBB	115,182	124,586	30,899	31,596	32,340	10,791	10,815	..
Non–EU balance on trade in goods (£m)	LGDT	−31,912	−45,598	−12,259	−12,567	−11,736	−3,903	−3,898	..
Non–EU exports of goods (excl oil & erratics)[5]	SHDJ	119.8	118.0	111.6	112.5	115.2	118.4	109.6	..
Non–EU imports of goods (excl oil & erratics)[5]	SHED	116.8	124.4	122.9	127.6	127.1	132.5	127.8	..
Non–EU import and price index (excl oil)[5]	LKWQ	101.2	103.9	103.4	103.2	104.4	105.3	104.1	..
Non–EU export and price index (excl oil)[5]	LKVX	100.1	101.5	101.2	100.2	101.9	102.5	101.9	..
Monetary conditions/government finances									
M0 (year on year percentage growth)	VQMX	5.1	..	..	..	..	..	..	..
M4 (year on year percentage growth)	VQJW	11.3	13.3	14.4	12.8	12.9	12.9	13.3	..
Public sector net borrowing (£m)	−ANNX	40,789	33,226	6,167	12,999	−3,471	7,994	1,236	8,212
Net lending to consumers (£m)	RLMH	19,746	13,120	3,004	3,302	2,323	692	449	842

External indicators – non–ONS statistics

		2006 Oct	2006 Nov	2006 Dec	2007 Jan	2007 Mar	2007 Apr	2007 May	2007 June
Activity and expectations									
CBI output expectations balance	ETCU	9	5	11	12	21	18	18	25
CBI optimism balance	ETBV	−10			−7		16		
CBI price expectations balance	ETDQ	11	23	8	11	19	14	26	19

Notes:

1 Not seasonally adjusted.
2 Annual data are for April except for workforce jobs (June), claimant count (average of the twelve months) and vacancies (average of the four quarters).
3 Monthly data for vacancies and average earnings are averages of the three months ending in the month shown. Monthly data for all other series except
   claimant count are averages of the three months centred on the month shown.
4 FBTP: food, beverages, tobacco and petroleum.
5 Volumes, 2003 = 100.

For further explanatory notes, see Notes to tables on page 64.

Independent forecasts

June 2007

UK forecasts

The tables below supplement the Economic Review by providing a forward-looking view of the UK economy. The tables shows the average and range of independent forecasts for 2007 and 2008 and are extracted from HM Treasury's Forecasts for the UK Economy.

2007

	Average	Lowest	Highest
GDP growth (per cent)	2.7	2.2	3.1
Inflation rate (Q4, per cent)			
CPI	2.1	1.4	2.9
RPI	3.7	2.9	4.3
Claimant unemployment (Q4, million)	0.91	0.81	1.10
Current account (£ billion)	−42.8	−62.0	−29.0
Public Sector Net Borrowing (2007–08, £ billion)	35.2	25.3	41.0

2008

	Average	Lowest	Highest
GDP growth (per cent)	2.4	−0.3	3.0
Inflation rate (Q4, per cent)			
CPI	2.0	1.5	3.0
RPI	2.7	1.8	3.9
Claimant unemployment (Q4, million)	0.94	0.71	1.25
Current account (£ billion)	−44.6	−68.8	−25.4
Public Sector Net Borrowing (2008–09, £ billion)	33.8	19.4	44.5

Notes

Forecast for the UK economy gives more detailed forecasts, covering 32 variables, and is published monthly by HM Treasury. It is available on the Treasury's website at: www.hm-treasury.gov.uk/economic_data_and_tools/data_index.cfm

Selected world forecasts

The tables below supplement the Economic Review by providing a forward-looking view of the world economy. The tables show forecasts for a range of economic indicators taken from Economic Outlook (preliminary edition), published by OECD (Organisation for Economic Co-operation and Development).

2007

	US	Japan	Euro area	Total OECD
Real GDP growth (per cent)	2.1	2.0	2.5	2.6
Consumer price (percentage change from previous year)	2.6	−0.3	2.0	2.3
Unemployment rate (per cent of the labour force)	4.7	3.7	6.9	5.6
Current account (as a percentage of GDP)	−6.1	4.8	0.4	−1.5
Fiscal balance (as a percentage of GDP)	−2.8	−2.7	−0.8	−1.8

2008

	US	Japan	Euro area	Total OECD
Real GDP growth (per cent)	2.6	2.2	2.2	2.7
Consumer price (percentage change from previous year)	2.2	0.4	2.1	2.0
Unemployment rate (per cent of the labour force)	4.9	3.6	6.6	5.4
Current account (as a percentage of GDP)	−6.2	5.4	0.4	−1.5
Fiscal balance (as a percentage of GDP)	−2.8	−3.2	−0.7	−1.9

Notes

The OECD *Economic Outlook* is published bi-annually. Further information about this publication can be found at www.oecd.org/eco/Economic_Outlook

Dawn Camus
Office for National Statistics

FEATURE

Publishing productivity measures in ONS

SUMMARY

This July 2007 *Economic & Labour Market Review* (ELMR) is a special productivity edition and is published alongside *The ONS Productivity Handbook: A Statistical Overview and Guide*. Presenting all Office for National Statistics (ONS) productivity estimates, sources, methods and analysis, this single volume will serve as a valuable reference on the subject. Articles printed in this edition of ELMR have been chosen to complement the new handbook and provide new results from within ONS alongside views from outside the office. This article comments on the joint publication launch and what readers can gain from it.

What is productivity and why does it matter? The Office for National Statistics (ONS) has produced productivity measures for many years, including detailed figures for UK regions and estimates for some industries. These measures include long-standing whole economy estimates but also newly-developed market sector and public service figures. *The ONS Productivity Handbook* brings all these different measures together within a consistent framework, so that users are aware of the full range available. It also describes the methodology and data series used and discusses the issues arising.

This joint launch also marks the start of a new, annual productivity series – multi-factor productivity (MFP) estimates. Peter Goodridge's article presents estimates for the years 1997 to 2005, aiming towards a better understanding of the UK's productivity performance and, in turn, a better interpretation of the performance of the UK economy. One of the input series for MFP, the volume index of capital services (VICS), is also updated in this issue of ELMR in an article by Gavin Wallis.

While ONS produces a large number of productivity measures and analyses, its responsibilities are as much about providing data building blocks for others to carry out their own studies. The article by Jonathan Haskel, Professor of Economics at Queen Mary, University of London, discusses issues surrounding measurement of the services sector and the changing structure of the economy, using ONS data as a basis for his research. Martin Weale, Director

of the National Institute of Economic and Social Research (NIESR), focuses on measuring public services, commenting on the recent work by the UK Centre for the Measurement of Government Activity (UKCeMGA) and the future challenges it will face. As productivity is an area of rapid change, so must the outputs of the office reflect this and stay under constant review.

The past productivity approach

The first ONS Productivity Strategy (Lau, 2002) was drawn up following a consultation with users during the last months of 2001. It identified three main areas that were regarded as a priority for development:

- services sector productivity (including public sector productivity)
- investment and capital stock data, and
- skills and productivity

In the following four years, ONS tackled all these areas and made large-scale improvements. Other changes also took place, including a full review on the measurement of government output and productivity (Atkinson, 2005). In chronological order, there were a number of key developments:

- February 2002 – 'Labour productivity measures for the non-production industries' (Daffin, Reed and Vaze, 2002) was published. This investigation determined the services industries for which productivity estimates could be produced. Following this, publication of a new quarterly experimental release containing services sector productivity, 'Labour productivity indices for the non-production industries', began

■ April 2002 – the productivity strategy was published (Lau, 2002)

■ December 2003 – the National Statistician asked Sir Tony Atkinson to carry out an independent review of the measurement of government output in the National Accounts

■ July 2004 – a methodology review of productivity (Barnes and Williams, 2004) was published. This included documentation of productivity definitions and a new headline aggregate: output per worker

■ January 2005 – the Atkinson Review – Final Report, Measurement of government output and productivity (Atkinson, 2005) – was published

■ July 2005 – UKCeMGA was launched to take forward the recommendations from the Atkinson Review. Its aim was to strengthen the capability of ONS to publish authoritative and coherent measures of the output and productivity of government-provided services in the UK National Accounts

■ November 2005 – a volume index of capital services (Wallis, 2005) and a quality-adjusted labour input measure (Holmwood, Lau, Richardson and Wallis, 2005) were launched. These experimental series, required for producing MFP estimates, are updated annually. The latest update of VICS is included in this edition of ELMR

By July 2006, when a second, updated productivity strategy was published (Camus and Lau, 2006), the productivity measures and related data produced by ONS had changed considerably. The headline measure had changed, there were services productivity estimates, new series for productivity in public services were being developed, and experimental series required for MFP estimates were being produced annually. In the background, data sources used by ONS for National Accounts and labour market statistics were also improving.

These changes had another effect. Where there had been one Productivity First Release, there was now a large array of productivity measures. These measures were published in different places and users were not always aware of them all. So, in early 2006, the proposal for a handbook was made.

The ONS Productivity Handbook

A Statistical Overview and Guide

The ONS Productivity Handbook

ONS set out to produce a handbook that would, for the first time, provide users with a single reference publication for all ONS productivity estimates, sources, methods and analysis. The new handbook meets this goal, and additional advantages include:

■ readers will now be better informed about the range and scope of ONS productivity work

■ gaps in productivity work will be more easily identifiable

■ areas of future co-operation, both internal and external, will be easier to identify

■ productivity work carried out by ONS will gain increased publicity

The chapters have been selected to reflect every aspect of productivity work within ONS and each chapter was written by the experts in the relevant area. Planned to cover everything that a practitioner would want to know about ONS productivity measures, the book provides this information in the words of those producing them. Topics range from the data series required to construct productivity measures to the detailed methodology used, from figures and methods used at regional level to international comparisons. There are also contributions from other government departments (Department of Trade and Industry, HM Treasury) giving the viewpoint of users, for example,

details of the five drivers of productivity. Additionally, the Organisation for Economic Co-operation and Development kindly provided a section on international comparisons of productivity to set the UK measures in context. Finally, future plans are referred to in every section and detailed in the final chapter.

The future for ONS productivity measurement

The Quarterly National Accounts First Release, containing headline data to be published in the *Blue Book* 2007 was published on 29 June 2007. These new National Accounts include software investment for the first time. On 2 July, the Productivity First Release and a new quarterly data set of market sector productivity measures were published which also contained these investment figures for the first time. Then on 3 July, the results of the consultation carried out by UKCeMGA were published, providing details of how ONS plans to treat public services productivity in the future.

Productivity measurement in ONS continues to change and improvements continue to be made. As Martin Weale comments in his article, while much progress has been made in enhancing measures of output and input for public services, particularly for individually consumed public services, there is still a substantial amount of work to do. Results from the recent consultation will be used by

UKCeMGA to advance the public services agenda.

Jonathan Haskel comments that the incorporation of software is a welcome step forward, but there is still much more that can be done to improve measurement of services sector productivity, particularly in the areas of research and development (R&D) and intangibles. ONS is already involved in project work on both these topics and some results have already been published on R&D in ELMR (Edworthy and Wallis, 2007) and by Queen Mary, University of London on intangibles (Giorgio Marrano, Haskel and Wallis, 2007).

That said, what productivity is will not change. It will always require measurements of output from the National Accounts and measurements of labour, capital and other inputs. Users will still be interested in figures for regional comparisons, for international comparisons and at as detailed an industry level as possible. *The ONS Productivity Handbook* should be an excellent guide to ONS productivity measures both today and for many years to come.

CONTACT

✉ elmr@ons.gsi.gov.uk

REFERENCES

Atkinson (2005) Atkinson Review: *Final Report, Measurement of government output and productivity* at
www.statistics.gov.uk/cci/nugget.asp?id=663

Barnes M and Williams M (2004) 'UK official productivity estimates: review of methodology', *Economic Trends* 610, pp 111–38 and at
www.statistics.gov.uk/cci/article.asp?id=935

Camus D and Lau E (2006) 'Productivity measures and analysis: ONS strategy and work programme', *Economic Trends* 632, pp 14–24 and at
www.statistics.gov.uk/cci/article.asp?id=1603

Daffin C, Reed G and Vaze P (2002) 'Labour productivity measures for the non-production industries', *Economic Trends* 579, pp 41–56 and at
www.statistics.gov.uk/cci/article.asp?id=144

Edworthy E and Wallis G (2007) 'Treating research and development as a capital asset', *Economic & Labour Market Review* 1(2), pp 16–25 and at
www.statistics.gov.uk/cci/article.asp?id=1724

Giorgio Marrano M, Haskel J and Wallis G (2007) 'What Happened to the Knowledge Economy? ICT, Intangible Investment and Britain's Productivity Record Revisited', Department of Economics, Queen Mary, University of London, Working Paper 603 and at
www.econ.qmul.ac.uk/papers/wp/wp603.htm

Holmwood R, Lau E, Richardson C and Wallis G (2005) 'An experimental quality-adjusted labour input measure', *Economic Trends* 624, pp 30–41 and at
www.statistics.gov.uk/cci/article.asp?id=1298

Lau E (2002) 'Productivity Measures: ONS strategy', *Economic Trends* 581, pp 20–5 and at
www.statistics.gov.uk/cci/article.asp?id=145

Wallis G (2005) 'Estimates of the volume of capital services', *Economic Trends* 624, pp 42–51 and at
www.statistics.gov.uk/cci/article.asp?id=1297

FEATURE

Martin Weale
National Institute of Economic and Social Research

Following the Atkinson Review: the quality of public sector output

SUMMARY

The UK Centre for the Measurement of Government Activity has made substantial progress in the measurement of public service output and inputs, publishing a series of productivity articles, but inevitably there is room for more work, particularly in the measurement of the quality of both outputs and inputs.

This article addresses two of the key issues raised by the Atkinson Review – quality adjustment and the use of value weights. The benefit of addressing quality issues in the context of conventional index number formulae is shown. This leads to smaller quality adjustments than some past work on public sector output has suggested. It is demonstrated that, without the use of value weights, it is not always possible to make quality adjustments. Nevertheless, where value weights cannot be based on market information, they may be difficult to identify and care will be needed in identifying changes to relative values.

Measurement of public sector activity in constant prices poses problems with no straightforward solutions. For many years it seemed to be the Cinderella of national income accounting. In the 1990s, considerable effort was devoted to the production of price and volume indices for the information technology sector, because of a feeling that simple price and volume indices greatly understated the growth of the industry. The public sector is considerably larger than the information technology sector. However, after some experimentation with activity measures, from the 1960s until the 1990s outputs were typically measured by means of rather crude indicators of inputs, such as numbers of people employed.

The 1993 System of National Accounts, followed by the 1995 European System of Accounts, proposed a move away from input indicators to activity indicators. Instead of counting the number of teachers in schools, one should count the number of children being taught. Health output might be measured by the number of patients treated and not the number of people employed by the health service. The UK, often in the lead in implementing new national accounting standards, started to move towards output-based measures in 1998. The effect was to depress estimates of economic growth to some extent.

There was a large increase in public spending between 1999 and 2005 and, at much the same time, the Government adopted a system of targets for public sector services in order to monitor and,

it was hoped, improve performance. It was therefore of particular concern that the National Accounts showed labour productivity in the public sector declining. In 2003 the National Statistician asked Sir Tony Atkinson to review the problems of measuring the output, and thus the productivity, of the public sector. The Review led to the setting up of the UK Centre for the Measurement of Government Activity (UKCeMGA) at the Office for National Statistics, as a way of implementing its proposals.

The Review produced nine principles. Key to these were the first two – that, as far as possible, public sector outputs should be treated in the same way as private sector outputs and that adjustments should be made for changes in quality. The Review also proposed that indices of individual components of output should be weighted together using value weights rather than cost weights. After summarising some of the work done since UKCeMGA was set up, this article focuses on these two intimately related questions.

Progress so far

UKCeMGA has looked so far at four areas: education, health, adult social care and social security administration. Its papers on the first two areas include estimates of the productivity performance of the sectors after making quality adjustments, while the papers on the final two areas discuss a number of possible indicators but do not yet provide any quantitative assessment of their implications. A strategy paper (ONS,

2007) published on 3 July 2007 consolidates this work and sets out plans for the future. It also provides details of specific decisions taken on measurement methods for health and education.

Measurement of productivity involves measurement of inputs and outputs and the contribution made by labour and capital. Construction of volume measures of value added requires the first two of these, although the UK has traditionally short-cut the issue by assuming that volume movements in gross output match volume movements in value added.

UKCeMGA has made substantial progress in the measurement of all of these questions, focusing on activity measures. This has largely involved increased distinction between the different types of activities carried out by components of the public sector. Thus, before there was substantial concern about volume measures for public sector activities, hospital output was measured by classifying each procedure into one of 16 activities. It is easy to believe that such a crude classification could result in substantial biases, and that a move to an index of some 1,600 activities is an improvement. On the other hand, care is needed to ensure that all the output of any sector is enumerated and this has led to a preference for calculating output indices for the market sector by deflating value measures rather than by collecting output volumes. The risk of activity-based measures neglecting new forms of activity may increase as the degree of disaggregation is increased.

Considerable effort has also been devoted to the measurement of factor inputs. Here, as in any productivity calculation, it is important to measure labour input after allowing for differential use of different types of labour rather than simply using a head count or a measure of total hours worked. If this is not done, changes in total factor productivity will be confused with changes in labour input. Similarly, attention needs to be given to the measurement of capital services, rather than reliance put on indices of the capital stock. In both of these areas UKCeMGA has achieved a great deal.

Inevitably, however, there is room for more work in the measurement of the quality of both outputs and, particularly in the case of the health service, inputs. The question of outputs is discussed below. On the issue of inputs, it is adequate to note that there has been substantial technical progress in the pharmaceutical industry in terms of capabilities of drugs available. There has, so far, been no attempt to produce

Table 1

Productivity estimates for components in the public sector, 2004

Indices (1999=100)

	Consistent with current National Accounts	After quality adjustment
Education	90	100
Health	93	98
Social security administration	82	
Adult social care	92	

quality-adjusted measures of the output of pharmaceutical industry and thus of the inputs bought in by the health service.

Table 1 shows the estimates of changes in public sector productivity produced by UKCeMGA after taking account of the quality effects which it has been able to identify. The results are only approximate, because the presentation of the estimates in the various papers from which they are drawn, and for which references are given in the table, is graphical. Thus, the numbers for 1999 and 2004 have to be read off the graphs. Nevertheless, the broad impression they give is adequate.

It has to be said that the results do not provide a flattering picture of public sector productivity performance. In fields of both education and health, the quality adjustments have made a substantial difference; there are, nevertheless, reasons for questioning whether the adjustments made have been appropriate and this issue is now explored.

Quality adjustment

The basic principle behind quality adjustment of the output of the public sector is the same as that elsewhere in the National Accounts – outputs of different quality should be treated as distinct outputs in the construction of quantity indices of output. Suppose that there are two qualities of output in period t, q_{1t} and q_{2t} with base-period unit values p_1 and p_2. Then the quality-adjusted Laspeyres output index comparing period t with period 1 is

$$I_t^q = \frac{p_1 q_{1t} + p_2 q_{2t}}{p_1 q_{11} + p_2 q_{21}} \text{ x } 100$$

This compares with the unadjusted index calculated if the output is assumed to be homogeneous

$$I_t^h = \frac{q_{1t} + q_{2t}}{q_{11} + q_{21}} \text{ x } 100$$

The same principle can of course be applied to the calculation of other types of index, such as the chain-linked index which is actually used in the National Accounts

nowadays.

A question to which the formula immediately gives rise is where the unit values come from to make the calculation possible. If output were marketed, they would of course be the market prices (or the market prices net of sales taxes). In the absence of a market, the most obvious choice is that the social values of the different outputs should be used. In some cases this may be very straightforward, and an application to education illustrates this very clearly.

Education

Suppose that the question is how to produce an index of education output which reflects changes in the quality of teaching and that this can be measured by exam results. Two quality categories are identified, children with 5+ GCSEs at grades A to C and those who have not reached this level. Suppose that the difference in the unit values of the two qualities of education is reflected in differences in earning power. Suppose also that, on average, a child with 5+ GCSEs earns 20 per cent more than one who does not cross this threshold (this is consistent with the figures produced by McIntosh (2006), although he identifies separately the value of lower levels of GCSE attainment). Then $p_1 = 1$ and $p_2 = 1.2$. If the proportion of children with 5+ GCSEs rises from 60 per cent to 63 per cent and the number of children is unchanged, it can be seen immediately that

$$I_t^q = \frac{1 \text{ x } 37 + 1.2 \text{ x } 63}{1 \text{ x } 40 + 1.2 \text{ x } 60} \text{ x } 100 = 100.5$$

while the homogeneous index shows no change. The outcome can also be compared with that proposed by the Department for Education and Skills (DfES, 2005), which recommends an index

$$I_t^d = \frac{63}{60} \text{ x } 100 = 105$$

Comparison of that with the formula for I_t^q shows that the latter would take a value of 105 only if the value put on children with no qualifications were zero or, which is an easier proposition to defend, if it were believed that their education had no effect on their earning power (something not supported by McIntosh's results since he shows earnings benefits from some success at GCSE for children who do not reach the 5 A to C grade threshold). While cases can be made for other valuation systems, the use of figures based on what is known about earning power is not likely to be controversial.

These calculations are not the whole of the matter since the exam scores of children currently taking GCSEs are presumably a function of the quality of their teaching throughout their time at school. Thus, there are serious issues to be resolved about the best way of allocating the quality effects over time. ONS (2007) sets out a programme of work to address this issue. But the general principle that quality adjustment can be seen as an index number issue is clear enough.

One final point should be made since there is some discussion among national accountants about whether value weights are more appropriate than cost weights (see below). In this example at least, cost weights would seem to be highly inappropriate. It is perfectly possible that teaching children who reach 5+ GCSEs is no more expensive than teaching children who do not cross the threshold. But this hardly implies that the extra education implied by the better exam result is of no use. One might also note that the use of value weights defined in this way is entirely consistent with the way in which labour force quality is measured in productivity calculations. On the other hand, one can reasonably be concerned if post-compulsory education is not valued unless the latter leads to enhanced earning power, otherwise it would neglect the consumption value of such courses and the knowledge derived from them to those who undertake them.

Ideally, instead of categorising children, the exam score of each would be identified and a measure of quality built from this. ONS (2007) proposes this approach in preference to the threshold measure described above. To apply the above principles, a unit value would need to be associated with each exam score. In practice, of course, it is unlikely that unit values will be able to be identified in this way.

Suppose, however, that the unit values are given as linear functions of the exam marks and the value p_s associated with a score of s is given as

$$p_s = a + b_s$$

Then, if $q_{s,t}$ is the number of children with score s in year t, the quality-adjusted index is

$$I_t^q = \frac{\sum_s (a+bs)q_{s,t}}{\sum_s (a+bs)q_{s,0}} \times 100 = \frac{(a+b/\bar{s}_t)\sum_s q_{s,t}}{(a+b/\bar{s}_0)\sum_s q_{s,0}} \times 100$$

where $\bar{s}_t$ is the average score in year t. The important point to note about this is that if $a>0$, a 1 percentage point improvement in exam score is associated with a less than 1 percentage point improvement in earning power. The use, proposed by ONS (2007), of ratio of average marks in different years as a means of quality adjustment will overstate the improvement which would be shown by the appropriate index number. (It is possible to imagine $a=0$ but harder to accept $a< 0$. The latter would imply that school subtracted value from children who performed badly in exams.) Unless there is a firm statistical basis for the function $p_s = a+bs$, it may well be better to rely on a rather small number of categories for which pay differentials and thus unit values can be derived. It should also be noted that if the value function is not linear in the exam score, then use of the mean is doubtful.

Health

The study of hospital output by Castellani et al (2007) provides another illustration of the problems arising in making quality adjustments. A reduction in the mortality rate associated with hospital treatment is plainly an improvement in quality. At present, for most in-patient treatments, it is possible to distinguish only two categories, patients who survive and those who do not. Values can be obtained for the two types of outputs by using, for the surviving patients, a measure of the increase in quality-adjusted life years and, for the dying patients, the quality-adjusted life years lost as a result of their treatment. Since there is very little information available on the benefits of different treatments, it is possible only to make rather arbitrary assumptions about the gains relative to the losses.

There are a number of difficult issues. If a treatment raises the welfare of a patient by a uniform amount for each remaining year of life, is the treatment of a young patient 'more output' than that of an old patient? It may seem sensible to treat the deaths of young patients as bigger losses than the deaths of old patients, but to assume that, for surviving patients, the amount of treatment is not dependent on their ages. On the other hand, if hospital treatment is seen as saving people who would have otherwise died, then no value is actually subtracted by patients' deaths. Ideally, as

proposed by ONS (2007), one would make a distinction between those patients who die as a result of their treatment (avoidable death) and those who die simply because their treatment does not work (unavoidable death). Of course, where the patient is provided with terminal care because nothing else can be done, that is in itself valuable and should not be treated in the same way as other unavoidable death.

The Department of Health (DH) has been keen to ensure that an index of output pays due regard to the quality of the patient experience with respect to the hotel services offered by hospitals. Here, problems arise similar to those involved in the measurement of school quality. Patient experience is measured by means of sample surveys of patients who are asked to report on a range of issues such as food quality, hospital cleanliness and staff politeness. The question then is how the unit values for various treatments should be adjusted upwards or downwards in the light of the patient scores.

Suppose that a particular treatment is identified (such as a hip replacement) with a unit value of p_j in terms of the medical benefits conferred by the treatment. The patient has also given a score of s for the non-medical aspects of the treatment. What then is the total value of the treatment to the patient and how would it change if the quality of the non-medical aspects changed? Suppose that one could identify a value to be put on the score, $v_j = a_j s$ (although there is no need for the relationship to be linear). The value on the score may well depend on the procedure in question, for example because the value put on a short waiting time is likely to depend on what the patient is waiting for.

This suggests a score-adjusted value of the treatment as

$$p_{j,s} = p_j + a_j s$$

where p_j is the unit value for treatment j for a surviving patient. It is plain that to apply this formula one has to decide, somehow or other, on the value for a_j. The measure adopted by DH avoided this problem by assuming that

$$p_{j,s} = s p_j$$

but it is very difficult to see a justification for this approach beyond the point that it avoids the need to take a view on what is in fact the key issue, the importance of non-medical quality relative to medical treatment, in treatment packages. ONS (2007) suggests that this issue will now be addressed.

These examples show the importance, when making quality adjustments, of starting with the basic principles lying behind index numbers. This leads naturally to the treatment of different qualities of output as output of different products with different unit values attached. It also leads to a consideration of the effects of quality on unit values. It is unlikely from work to date, either by the various government departments or, indeed, in the treatment of patient experience in the York/National Institute of Economic and Social Research study of hospital output, that the quality adjustments were approached from this perspective.

The issue of quality can blur into that of new products. For example, if a form of medical treatment is improved in terms of what it does for patients, then the treatment can be regarded as a new product with a unit value higher than that of the treatment it replaced. Provided that the unit value can be identified, then the calculation of the output index is quite straightforward.

Valuation issues

The Atkinson Review proposed that, where possible, value weights rather than cost weights should be used in the construction of the output indices described above. Thus, if the value of some particular product or activity to the private sector is believed to be higher than its cost of production, the importance of changes in this activity in an overall output measure will be enhanced compared with what would be produced by a cost-based output index.

The logic behind this is clear. In the private sector, an output index is calculated using the prices at which the goods produced are then sold, and not on the basis of their cost of production. The two are conventionally equated, because profit is calculated as the residual, although it is regarded as the cost of capital. Thus the calculation is clearly driven by sales values rather than any identifiable costs of production.

The National Accounts, at present, have the property that value of output equals cost of production, with profit being treated as a cost of production. This identity is the core of the accounting system. For the private sector, since profit is calculated as a residual by deducting other production costs from output value, the identity will always be met. But in the public sector, if output values are allowed to differ from costs of production, the key identity will be broken. Alternatively, some new income category will be needed to maintain the income/expenditure identity which is core

to current price National Accounts. Since the residual term in the existing National Accounts is called operating surplus, a possible name for the new type of income might be social surplus.

In some cases the derivation of the values of outputs may be reasonably straightforward. Thus, in the education example discussed above, there is a market for qualified labour and that market provides a measure of the value offered by education. In other cases there is no market, and appropriate means are needed to assess the values that people put on public services. Where this is possible, care is needed to deal with the point that different people value services differently. In the private sector, those consumers who value a service at or above its sale price buy the service, while those who value it less do not. The National Accounts do not measure the consumer surplus associated with the people who would be prepared to pay higher prices if they had to.

Many public sector outputs are goods or services which are provided because of need. Healthy people do not expect hip replacements and, of those who are treated, the expected benefit to some is probably greater than to others. Thus, the principle of marginal valuation needs to be amended to reflect the fact that, for many people, the good or service may be of no use at all. To apply the private sector principle, the service provided by the public sector should be valued on the basis of the value put on it by the marginal consumer, that is, the consumer who derives the least benefit from the treatment. Thus, if health treatment is valued more by a young person than an old one, because the former has a longer expected life, the social value would be given by the value of the treatment to the old person. In the same way, police protection might be valued more by high earners than low earners because the former may put higher values on their own lives. But the value used by the low earners would be that adopted in the National Accounts.

Illustration of the way in which this principle works clarifies a number of points which have confused at least this author. Suppose that, for reasons nothing to do with the health service, people live longer. The value they put on treatments such as cataract operations is likely to increase because they will be in a position to enjoy the benefits for longer. If the cost is unchanged and allocation is efficient, the number of people treated will rise to the point where the benefit enjoyed by the marginal patient is what it was before.

Has the volume index of cataract operations increased in line with the number of patients treated? Or has it increased more because the non-marginal patients are enjoying more quality-adjusted life years – a widely accepted measure of health outputs? The value of the treatment to the marginal patient does not change, even though more patients are treated. Marginal valuation therefore implies that changes in the number of operations (the activity measure) are therefore the appropriate guide to the change in output. Of course there is no guarantee that allocation of resources to cataract operations is efficient. But statisticians would probably be unhappy with a departure from the principles set out above on the grounds that too few or too many patients are treated. Should the value of the treatment to the marginal patient change because more or fewer patients are treated, that seems *prima facie* to be a price change rather than a quantity change. In practice, local variations in health services mean that a patient who would be treated in one area may be refused treatment in another area. Addressing this needs further thought but, in the short term, national accountants would probably feel most comfortable using the lowest of a possible range of marginal values, when these differ for geographic reasons.

This can be contrasted where the number of quality-adjusted life years associated with a medical procedure changes because of changes to the procedure or some other technical advance. In that case, the normal process would be to treat the improvement to the procedure as an improvement in quality which should be reflected in a volume index. Here, the proportionate increase in volume is probably best derived with reference to the patient who was marginal under the old procedure. The ratio of quality-adjusted life years for this patient under the new procedure relative to that under the old procedure gives the proportionate increase in volume. Thus, if the old procedure had not been applied to patients over the age of, say, 75 because of its cost, while the new procedure was worth providing to older patients, the volume index is derived from consideration of the 75 year old patient.

These principles no doubt need further elaboration. But the examples above demonstrate the importance of thinking about the impact on the marginal beneficiary of public spending. They also show that, while it is important to think about outcomes as well as activities, there are circumstances in which changes in activity measures are more appropriate than changes in outcome measures as indicators of output movement. Perhaps they also point to a principle which would probably be widely accepted that, if nothing happens in the production process of a public service, then the output index should remain unchanged even if, for some completely exogenous reason, the benefit derived from the service to the marginal consumer increases.

Conclusions

UKCeMGA has achieved a great deal in enhancing measures of input and output for individually consumed public services. Progress with collectively consumed services is likely to be harder. Even with individual services, as the discussion above suggests, there remains a considerable amount of conceptual clarification to be done there is a substantial amount of work to do in the way in which quality changes are treated and the author looks forward to seeing more progress in this area.

CONTACT

 elmr@ons.gsi.gov.uk

REFERENCES

Castelli A, Dawson D, Gravelle H, Jacobs R, Kind P, Loveridge P, Martin S, O'Mahony M, Street A, Stevens P, Stokes L and Weale M R (2007) 'A New Approach to Measuring Health System Output and Productivity', *National Institute Economic Review* No 200.

Department for Education and Skills (2005) 'Measuring Government Education Output in the National Accounts' at www.dfes.gov.uk/research/programme ofresearch/index.cfm?type=5

McIntosh S (2006) 'Further analysis of the returns to academic and vocational qualifications', *Oxford Bulletin of Economics and Statistics* Vol 68 pp 225–51.

Office for National Statistics (2007) 'Measuring Quality as a Part of Public Service Output' at www.statistics.gov.uk/cci/article.asp?id=1831

FEATURE

Jonathan Haskel
Queen Mary, University of London

Measuring innovation and productivity in a knowledge-based service economy

SUMMARY

This article provides a review of measurement conventions for the services sector and for investment in knowledge assets. It is widely argued that activity in modern-day economies is increasingly becoming concentrated in the services sector and in the form of spending on knowledge, assets like design software, training and research and development (R&D).

The article summarises recent work and concludes that productivity measurement in the services sector is not as unreliable as some have said but more needs to be done to incorporate knowledge assessment into measurement.

Are current measurement systems adequate to document and understand productivity? There are two main arguments to say that they are not, both stemming from the assertion that statistical systems have not kept pace with structural change in the economy. First, it is argued that the services sector has grown and that productivity in it is not well measured. Second, it is argued that the knowledge economy has grown and that measurement conventions have missed this altogether.[1] This article reviews both these arguments, drawing on recent work by academics and statistics agencies.

The services sector

Market services are around 42 per cent of gross domestic product (GDP), with public services about 22 per cent. One helpful generic way of thinking about services is to think of output as having the dimensions of quantity, space and time. Consumers clearly value the quantity of output for the stream of consumption services it yields. But consumers also presumably value the location of a good in terms of space and time. In terms of space, consumers value having goods readily available near them, hence the transportation and retailing industry. As for time, consumers wish to smooth consumption and producers to borrow money against future projects. This service is provided in part by the financial services industry, which holds savers' money safely and screens borrowers.

In some cases, of course, consumption and production cannot be separated in time

or space: haircuts, medical operations and teaching, for example. Thus Melvin (1990) defines services that overcome the time or space separation between consumers and producers as 'intermediation services'. This includes transport, retailing and some financial services. He defines 'contact services' as those that arise when production and consumption cannot be separated, for example, haircuts, education, medical and financial advice.

How does this help define output? The output of a shoe shipper who transports shoes from the manufacturer is not the shoes. Rather, it is the bundle of intermediation services involved in the transport of those shoes. Similarly, the output of the shoe retailer who sells the shoes on to the final consumer from the manufacturer is not the shoes themselves; rather, it is the bundle of retail services, such as ambience, assortment, and convenience to the shopper.

In contact services, such as education, since it is hard to separate consumption and production, there would be the temptation to measure the number of teachers, or number of bankers providing financial advice. But once again, what is being produced here is a bundle of services, in these cases education and advice.

At first sight, this complicates the problem, since a bundle of services, like advice, retailing services or transport would appear to be too intangible to measure (as opposed to the bundle of shoes produced by the shoe manufacturer). However, if the service is valuable, then someone should be willing to pay for it. The point should be obvious to anyone who has bought a bottle of wine in a restaurant and calculated the premium over what it would have cost at a nearby supermarket. This margin between the retail price consumers pay for a good and the wholesale cost of buying it in is, in a well-functioning market, a reflection of the valuation that consumers place on the bundle of services (in this case the ambiance of drinking wine in the restaurant).

The general approach of measuring the value of a service, given that many services are intermediation activities, is to measure the margin involved in providing that service. This has an obvious resonance in retailing and restaurants and can be simply applied to transport (here, the price charged for transport services is the margin, since no ownership changes hands).

One aspect of services is that providers can vary the level of service that they deliver and in many cases shift it to the consumer. An obvious example is self-service, in retailing, or restaurants; however, the margins measurement method is likely to be robust to this. A self-service restaurant is cheaper than a full-service one and this correctly reflects the smaller bundle of services that such a restaurant supplies. Another example is travel. Many people book their travel on the internet themselves, a powerful reflection of the shifting of a service almost entirely onto the consumer. Yet these prices are cheaper than going via travel agents, which correctly reflects the reduced service levels received.

If this method is used to work out the nominal value of the bundle of services offered, what can be said about the real value? The usual method of converting nominal (money) into real values is to collect data on the price of the good in question. However, with services, more care is required in some cases. If restaurants move to more self-service with, perhaps, worse ambience, then it will be important to make sure that collected prices are differentiated by restaurant type to account for this. Such a quality adjustment is not unknown for manufactured goods.

One area where there needs to be more progress, argued by Oulton (2004), is that while there are many price indices collected for manufacturing, the price indices for corporate services, which are much of services and 23 per cent of GDP, are thinner on the ground. Data for these service areas began in 1992. As Allsopp (2004, pp 63 and 64) reports, the Office for National Statistics (ONS) calculates and publishes 32 services

producer price indices, covering 55 per cent of corporate services. In contrast, price indices for 1,000 manufacturing products and price indices for around 250 four-digit manufacturing industries are published.

Recent developments in measurement of services, both improvements in coverage of price indices and the work underpinning designation of the Index of Services as a National Statistic, are outlined in Tily (2006) and in Drew and Morgan (2007).

There are clearly some areas where the margin approach is problematic. First, in many public services, there is no market that transacts the service from which a margin can be inferred. In a number of sectors therefore, the convention had grown up to measure the output by the input, for example, the number of doctors, or number of teachers. The ONS public sector measurement programme is designed in large part to confront this question.

Second, problems might also arise if transactions are priced, but bundled together. For example, many banks offer 'free' banking for a range of transactions. In reality of course, transactions are not free, but the price is bundled together with a range of other services. Bundling also occurs in other sectors, for example, mobile phone contracts, so this is not likely to be a problem just confined to financial services.

A third problem is double-deflation[2] of margins requiring data on both the prices of outputs and inputs. Since in many sectors, for example, retailing, the margin is a relatively small number arising from the difference between two relatively large numbers, inaccurate price indices can result in seriously biased double-deflated margins.

One area where the margins approach has been applied is in the financial intermediation industry. As set out in Akritidis (2007), under standard national income accounting conventions, interest payments are not regarded as payments for a productive service. This is because production is defined as an activity involving labour and capital in which inputs become outputs and so factor incomes are generated. Lending, according to this view, is not such an activity. In a bank, the major sources of income are explicit charges for services and interest earned. In practice, however, explicit charges are small. So, value added, which by convention is the explicit charges, less intermediate input costs of running the bank (heating, stationery, and so on), is typically negative.

Under the new national accounts conventions, the value of financial services is inferred from a margin. The idea is that

at least some of the services provided by a bank, for example unpriced transactions and safekeeping of money, are revealed implicitly by the margin between interest payments received and what would be earned in some risk-free environment outside a bank. So, for example, payment made by banks on deposits with instant access is typically less than long-term savings payments, and this margin presumably reveals the services that a customer values of having their money instantly. Equally, the margin between the interest payment made by a consumer on a loan and the risk-free rate is a proxy for the services that consumers are willing to pay for to get the facility of the loan.

The knowledge economy

When European leaders met at the March 2000 Lisbon summit, they set the European Union the goal of becoming 'the most dynamic and competitive knowledge-based economy in the world' by 2010. The Spring European Council of 22–23 March 2005 placed renewed focus on growth, innovation and employment and in particular on supporting knowledge and innovation. Consider the following quote from this document:

> Knowledge is a critical factor with which Europe can preserve its international competitive advantage… Greater and more efficient investment in knowledge and innovation is needed… (EU, 2005)

Whatever the realism or otherwise of these goals, it clearly places the 'knowledge economy' in the forefront of policy interest and it sets out a number of objectives in terms of raising investment in knowledge. Therefore (at least) two questions might reasonably be asked. First, how is such investment in knowledge measured? Second, if there were to be more investment, how would that show up in measures of competitiveness? The way to begin addressing these questions is by considering research and development (R&D).

Knowledge investment in research and development

The prime focus of the Lisbon Agenda is R&D spending, with a specific target of 3 per cent for R&D spending as a fraction of GDP. So how is R&D spending measured? R&D spending data are collected fairly consistently across EU countries by official surveys that rely on the Frascati manual.

The key point here is that R&D is of a particular form, essentially scientific R&D. Therefore, for example, financial services typically do zero-measured R&D. Nor are any marketing activities related to R&D, such as market research in order to develop a product, allowed as R&D.

The emphasis on scientific knowledge is set out in the definitions of R&D spending that qualifies for tax credit, HMRC (2007a). They are worth considering in some detail. They say that an R&D project which seeks, for example, to:

- extend overall knowledge or capability in a field of science or technology
- create a process, material, device, product or service which incorporates or represents an increase in overall knowledge or capability in a field of science or technology
- make an appreciable improvement to an existing process, material, device, product or service through scientific or technological changes, or
- use science or technology to duplicate the effect of an existing process, material, device, product or service in a new or appreciably improved way (for example, a product which has exactly the same performance characteristics as existing models, but is built in a fundamentally different manner)

will be R&D for tax purposes if the project seeks to achieve an advance in overall knowledge or capability in a field of science or technology, not a company's own state of knowledge or capability alone.

A number of interesting points emerge from this. First, the emphasis on science[3] is clear. To make this point further, the guidelines give an example of what is not R&D (HMRC, 2007b). These examples are items such as:

- commercial and financial steps for innovation, development or marketing of an innovation
- work to develop non-scientific or non-technological aspects of an innovation
- the production and distribution of goods and services
- administration and other supporting services
- general support services (such as transportation, storage, cleaning, repair, maintenance and security)

A second point to notice is that the final sentence in the generic project detailed above requires that the R&D spending will bring benefits outside the firm, not just within the firm. This is a suitable criterion for giving a tax credit, since it requires that the social returns exceed the private returns. The definition of R&D in the Frascati manual does not specify this criterion and so is slightly broader. There are, of course, sound reasons for a narrow definition, since it aids compatibility and also accuracy. It might well be also that to the extent public policy is interested in spillovers from R&D, such spillovers are confined to scientific R&D.

Suppose, however, that this measure of R&D is considered correct and as accurately capturing knowledge spending in the economy. What then are the consequences for GDP of economies spending more on R&D? Conceptually, the way to think of this is that if output is due to increases in inputs, and one of those inputs is the knowledge stock, then the knowledge stock rises and output rises by the elasticity of output to the input, in this case the knowledge stock. Thus output has risen and investment has risen. Labour productivity has risen, but multi-factor productivity (MFP) has remained the same, since the increase in output is due to an increase in inputs.

There are, however, a number of measurement conventions that prevent these from being apparent in measured data. From this viewpoint, the main issue is that, under current conventions, R&D is not measured as an investment, but rather as an intermediate. Therefore any measured increase in value added (due to the unmeasured increase in the knowledge stock that enables firms to make cheaper or more desirable goods) is entirely due to MFP, since all that has happened is a rise in intermediate spending. Indeed, as the economy becomes more knowledge-intensive, investment rates will tend to fall.

This treatment of R&D has been widely argued to be inconsistent. If intangible spending does create a long-lived asset, then it should also be treated as investment and so should affect output. Indeed, Hill and Youngman (2002) argued it was conceptually correct to include intangibles as investment and pointed out that current SNA treatment was somewhat inconsistent. So, for example, mineral prospecting expenditure, that generates knowledge about new mineral deposits, is treated as investment. More recently, software, both purchased and own-account has also been treated as investment.

Consequently a number of questions arise. First, what spending on intangibles might be treated as creating long-lived assets? In particular, should R&D or other measures be used? Second, if such spending is treated as capital and not intermediate expenses, then what are the effects on GDP?

The categories of spending on knowledge building have been discussed by in a series of papers by Corrado, Hulten and Sichel (2005, 2006) and Nakamura (1999, 2001, 2003), who also try to quantify such spending for the US. They argue that R&D, in the sense of investing in knowledge, is much broader than just scientific R&D. For example, it could be argued that employer-spending on training is R&D in staff (and like scientific R&D in products, may or may not succeed and may or may not stay within the firm). Or, spending on market research is as much knowledge investment as is spending on the technical details of developing the machine itself. Therefore Corrado, Hulten and Sichel classify spending on intangibles into three categories:

- computerised information (mainly software)
- innovative property (mainly scientific and non-scientific R&D, the latter including design), and
- firm competencies (company spending on reputation capital, human capital and organisational capital)

These categories are all designed to capture dimensions of investment in knowledge assets. Regarding the first category, the computer age has naturally changed the face of tangible investment, via hardware, but the merest casual inspection suggests that spending on software is just as likely to be important, if not more so. As for the second category, this is designed to capture spending on knowledge-building of innovative property of the firm, while the last category is expenditure on the competencies of an organisation that make it more than the mere sum of the employee headcount.

Giorgio Marrano and Haskel (2006) have attempted to calculate investment in these categories for the UK and their results are set out in **Table 1**. The top section show expenditure on computerised information, amounting to nearly £22 billion, which is 18 per cent of total intangible investment. The second section shows R&D and non-scientific R&D. R&D itself is about one-third of this total category and 10 per cent of total intangible investment (note that software is 18 per cent of total intangible spending). New architectural and engineering designs are 15 per cent of total spending, but these are very much guesstimates since it is so hard to quantify innovation here. More work is clearly needed in this area. Finally, around 50 per

Table 1

Intangibles, 2004

	Type of intangible investment	Data source	Total spending (£ billion)	Percentage of total intangible investment[1]
	Computerised information			
1	Computer software and databases	ONS estimates	21.6	18
	Innovative property			
2	Scientific R&D	Current expenditure on R&D from BERD.[2] R&D in computer industry subtracted	12.4	10
3	Mineral exploration	National Accounts	0.4	0
4	Copyright and licence costs	National Accounts	2.4	2
5	New product development costs in the financial industry	20% of all intermediate purchase by financial services industry, ONS data	6.0	5
6	New architectural and engineering designs	Half of the total turnover of the architecture and design industry SIC[3] 742, ABI[4] data, plus twice the turnover of speciality design activities SIC 74782	18.0	15
7	R&D in social science and humanities		0.3	0
8	Total (2+3+4+5+6+7+8)		39.5	32
	Economic competencies			
9	Advertising expenditure	Total spending on advertising as reported by Advertising Association, less expenditure on classified ads	14.0	7
10	Market research	Twice revenues of the market and consumer research industry, ABI[4]	4.5	2
11	Firm-specific human capital	NESS05[5], a survey of employer-provided training	28.8	24
12	Organisational structure: purchased	Revenues of management consulting industry from Management Consulting Association	7.0	5
13	Organisational structure: own-account	20% of value of executive time (using executive wages from ASHE[6])	15.3	13
14	Total (9+10+11+12+13)		69.6	50
15	Grand total		130.7	100

Notes:

1 It is assumed that 60 per cent of '10' and '11' and 80 per cent of '13' are intangible investment.
2 Business Enterprise Research and Development.
3 Standard Industrial Classification.
4 Annual Business Inquiry.
5 National Employer Skills Survey.
6 Annual Survey of Hours and Earnings.

Source: Giorgio Marrano, Haskel and Wallis (2007)

cent of total investment is on firm spending on reputation, human and organisational capital (economic competencies).

One feature to emerge from Table 1 is that some of these investments are counted as part of GDP in the UK National Accounts, for example, mineral exploration and copyright and licence costs. Recent National Accounts have also incorporated these as GDP software, although not all own-account software has been so incorporated. The US is aiming to incorporate R&D as an investment by 2009.

What then is the effect on GDP of assuming these categories as investment?

This is investigated in Giorgio Marrano, Haskel and Wallis (2007). The main findings follow naturally from the argument above. First, market sector gross value added (MGVA) is understated by about 13 per cent in 2004 and 6 per cent in 1970. This follows from treating spending on intangibles as investment so that GVA rises. Second, instead of the nominal business investment/MGVA ratio falling since 1970, it has been rising. Third, the growth of intangible investment has been sufficient to raise labour productivity growth over the 1990s, although it has fallen between 2000 and 2004.

Conclusion

Changes in the nature of the economy require statistical agencies to change measurement. This article has highlighted two particular cases. First, the growth of the services sector requires development of more price indices on services, as is in train. Second, the shift of investment to more knowledge assets requires consideration of how these might be incorporated into the SNA. Software has now been fully incorporated in UK GDP, and ONS has helped to head international research on the treatment of R&D. The research on intangibles outlined here shows the importance of continuing this work. It also provides a broad scale map of the ground that needs to be covered.

Notes

1 Two other arguments are often heard. First, that productivity is poorly measured in the government sector and that this therefore renders GDP per labour input inaccurate as a productivity measure (because, for example, output in the government sector is measured using inputs; previous UK measurement conventions used the number of teachers as an output measure in education). Second, that due to other factors such as pollution and psychological well-being, economic output is not a good measure of societal welfare and so output per head is not a meaningful welfare measure.

2 Double-deflation is a method to estimate real GVA by deflating output and intermediate inputs separately before subtracting the latter from the former. This is in contrast to the single deflation method whereby the subtraction is done at current prices and the difference (that is, GVA at current prices) is deflated using an output deflator to arrive at real GVA estimates. This means that an industry's gross output is deflated by the price of its output, while each input is deflated by its own price index.

3 Science is further defined in the guidelines. 'Science is the systematic study of the nature and behaviour of the physical and material universe. Work in the arts, humanities and social sciences, including economics, is not science for the purpose of these guidelines. Mathematical techniques are frequently used in science, but mathematical advances in and of themselves are not science unless they are advances in representing the nature and behaviour of the physical and material universe.'

ACKNOWLEDGEMENTS

Financial support for this research comes from HM Treasury and from the ESRC/EPSRC Advanced Institute of Management Research, grant number RES-331-25-0030, and was carried out at CeRiBA at the Business Data Linking Branch at ONS; I am grateful to all institutions concerned for their support. I thank Dawn Camus, Tony Clayton and Geoff Tily for very helpful comments. Errors and opinions are my own.

CONTACT

 elmr@ons.gsi.gov.uk

REFERENCES

Akritidis L (2007) 'Improving the measurement of banking services in the UK National Accounts', *Economic & Labour Market Review* 1(5), pp 29–37 and at www.statistics.gov.uk/cci/article.asp?id=1761

Allsopp Review, available at www.hm-treasury.gov.uk./consultations_and_legislation/allsopp_review/consult_allsopp_index.cfm

Corrado C, Hulten C and Sichel D (2005) 'Measuring Capital and Technology: An Expanded Framework', in *Measuring Capital in the New Economy*, edited by C Corrado, J Haltiwanger and D Sichel, National Bureau of Economic Research Studies in Income and Wealth, Vol. 65, pp 11–45, The University of Chicago Press, Chicago and London.

Corrado C, Hulten C and Sichel D (2006) 'Intangible Capital and Economic Growth', NBER Working Paper, No. 11948.

Drew S and Morgan D (2007) 'The launch of the Index of Services as a National Statistic', *Economic & Labour Market Review* 1(3), pp 39–46 and at www.statistics.gov.uk/cci/article.asp?id=1741

European Union (2005) 'Communication from the Commission to the Council and the European Parliament' at www.ec.europa.eu/growthandjobs/pdf/COM2005_330_en.pdf

Giorgio Marrano M and Haskel J (2006) 'How Much Does the UK Invest in Intangible Assets?', CEPR Discussion Paper No. 6287.

Giorgio Marrano M, Haskel J and Wallis G (2007) 'What Happened to the Knowledge Economy? ICT, Intangible Investment and Britain's Productivity Record Revisited', Queen Mary College, Economics Department Working Paper 603 and at www.econ.qmul.ac.uk/papers/wp/WP603.HTM

Hill T P, Youngman R (2002) ' The measurement of intangiblies in macroeconomic statistics' at www.euintangiblies.net

HM Revenue and Customs (2007a) 'R&D for tax purposes' at www.hmrc.gov.uk/randd/index.htm

HM Revenue and Customs (2007b) 'further guidelines' at www.hmrc.gov.uk/manuals/cirdmanual/CIRD81900.htm

Melvin J (1990) 'Time and Space in Economic Analysis', Canadian Journal of Economics, 23, pp 725–47, November, 1990.

Nakamura L (1999) 'Intangibles: what to put the *New* in the New economy?', Federal Reserve Bank of Philadelphia *Business review* (July/August): 3–16.

Nakamura L (2001) 'What is the US Gross Investment in Intangibles? (At least) One Trillion Dollars a Year!', Federal Reserve Bank of Philadelphia Working paper No 01–15.

Nakamura L (2003) 'The Rise in Gross Investment in Intangible Asset Since 1978', mimeo, Federal Reserve Bank of Philadelphia.

Oulton N (2004) 'A Statistical Framework for the Analysis of Productivity and Sustainable Development' at www.hm- treasury.gov.uk./consultations_and_legislation/allsopp_review/consult_allsopp_index.cfm

Tily G (2006) 'Improvements to timely measures of service sector output', *Economic Trends* 630, pp 29–42 and at www.statistics.gov.uk/cci/article.asp?id=1555

Wang C (2003) 'Loanable Funds, Risk and Bank Service Output', Federal Reserve Bank of Boston Paper 03–4 at www.bos.frb.org/economic/econbios/wang.htm.

Multi-factor productivity analysis

Peter Goodridge
Office for National Statistics

SUMMARY

This article presents multi-factor productivity, sometimes referred to as total factor productivity or growth accounting, results for 1997 to 2005 using an experimental quality-adjusted labour input measure and experimental estimates of capital services growth as inputs. The analysis has been produced for the whole economy and some broad industry groupings, with the aim of better understanding the UK's productivity performance over this period and of using the results as a diagnostic check on the consistency of output and input data.

Publication of multi-factor productivity (MFP) estimates, as a new annually-updated data set, is an important development for productivity analysis in the Office for National Statistics (ONS). This is because the framework applied – called the growth-accounting framework – provides a better understanding of the causes of output growth. It shows how much of this growth is due to growth in labour, for example by increasing the workforce or its quality, and how much by growth in capital, for example by making more use of machinery or other forms of capital. The residual of output growth that cannot be explained by growth in these inputs is referred to as MFP.

This residual is generally thought of as a measure of technical change but can also capture other effects that affect growth in output. These can include improvements in management techniques and processes, improvements in skill levels in the workforce not captured by the quality adjustment of labour, and intangibles such as brand equity, firm-specific human capital and organisational structure.

For the time period examined (1997 to 2005), roughly three-quarters of the output growth in the UK economy is due to changes in labour and capital; these are responsible in roughly equal proportion. The measures of labour and capital that have been used in these MFP calculations capture more accurately the input of labour and capital in the production process, giving a more precise picture of what has been driving output growth over this period. Due to how the measures of inputs have been developed,

these new MFP estimates also give an insight into features such as the importance of skills in the labour force. The MFP estimates illustrate how much of output growth has been caused by labour that has been adjusted for quality, while the decomposition of labour productivity gives a direct estimate of the contribution of labour composition (quality), which is an area of interest for analysts.

This article presents MFP results for the period 1997 to 2005. The work is a result of the ONS strategy on productivity first published in April 2002 (Lau, 2002) and revised in August 2006 (Camus and Lau, 2006). The inputs used for this analysis are the experimental quality-adjusted labour input measure (QALI) and the volume index of capital services (VICS). Detail on the methodology and calculation of the input data can be found in Goodridge (2006) for QALI, and Wallis (2005) and Wallis (2007) for VICS.

Details of the analysis

The analysis uses QALI and VICS alongside a measure of gross value added (GVA) to decompose output growth into the contributions of growth in inputs and growth in the residual, the latter being MFP. The same method is used to decompose labour productivity growth into growth in physical capital deepening, growth in labour composition and growth in MFP. The analysis is limited to six broad industry sectors due to the constraints of the QALI input data (Goodridge, 2006).

Part of the interest in MFP lies in the increase in use of information and communication technology (ICT) and its spillover effects, which are frequently proposed as an explanation for the acceleration in the productivity performance of the USA in the 1990s. Observers of this phenomenon are interested to know whether the UK has experienced any such surge in productivity growth as a result of increased use of ICT. As well as hardware – physical ICT capital – there has been considerable growth in investment in software, both purchased and own-account (developed in-house by the firm).

Software is an intangible asset, that is, an asset that does not have a physical, material existence. It is one of the few intangible assets included in National Accounts investment figures, although it will soon be joined by research and development (R&D) investment. Other intangible assets are not included in estimates of capital, mainly because of their nature and the difficulty in measuring them. Such assets are brand equity, firm-specific human capital, organisational capital and non-scientific R&D. Since investment in these categories is not measured, their contribution will also be present in the MFP residual. However, there is now a body of work attempting to measure such investments and investigate their productivity effects (see, for example, Giorgio Marrano, Haskel, and Wallis, 2007).

MFP analysis is also a useful tool for checking the consistency of output and input data and identifying measurement issues in these areas. For instance, a persistent decline in MFP growth is not compatible with a sector that is consistently growing in terms of its output. This is particularly relevant to service sector industries, especially financial intermediation and business services, and also the public sector, where output is believed to be underestimated due to the inherent measurement difficulties in these sectors. It is these sectors where quality improvement in output is most prevalent, but also most difficult to capture in official output data.

The analysis suggests negative MFP growth in, among others, the public and personal services sectors. This may be due to the failure to capture changes in quality in these sectors.

Another area of interest, particularly in relation to government policy, is the contribution of skills to productivity growth. Skills are listed as one of the five key drivers of productivity by the Department of Trade and Industry and it is part of government policy to improve

the skill level of the UK workforce and thus help reduce the productivity gap with the US and other industrialised nations. The results in this article estimate the contribution of skills by producing two sets of MFP results based on quality-adjusted and standard hours worked, and also by estimating the contribution of labour composition to labour productivity growth.

The results in this article differ from those published in Lau and Vaze (2002) in a number of ways. Firstly, they are produced at a slightly different industry breakdown. Secondly, the quality adjustment process is more detailed. Rather than adjusting for two sexes, three education levels and six industries, in this analysis, labour is adjusted for two sexes, eight education levels, six industries and six age groups. Finally, the output data (GVA) are compatible with *Blue Book* 2006 rather than *Blue Book* 2001 and have therefore been subject to revision, and of course so have nominal GVA, QALI, VICS and their components. However, as in the article by Lau and Vaze (2002), the output measure used has not been subject to any adjustment (for coherence or balancing). Also, a slightly different method is employed for calculating the income shares that accrue to both capital and labour. This is discussed in further detail later.

Growth accounting

MFP analysis, or growth accounting, apportions growth in output to growth in the factor inputs, capital and labour, and growth in a residual which represents disembodied technical change (the A term in equation 1 below), also sometimes known as the Hicks-neutral shift parameter (Bell, Burriel-Llombart and Jones, 2005). Therefore, if the growth rate of output is greater than the growth rate of the combined factor inputs, capital and labour, then the residual can be interpreted as an approximation of growth in disembodied technical change, that is, advances in technology not embodied in capital. Examples of such a change are increased knowledge through R&D or improvements in organisational structure or management. In general, it captures any improvement in output that is not captured in the data on the factor inputs.

In a sense, MFP growth can be thought of as increased efficiency. This can be achieved in a number of different ways. For instance, if a firm changes its organisational structure and this results in increased efficiency, then this can be thought of as MFP. The increase

in productivity is not due to an increase in the quantity or quality of capital but instead an improvement in how they are employed. Note that there has, however, been an increase in organisational capital but such investments are not considered in this analysis as they are not considered to be an investment in the current System of National Accounts. For further discussion of such investments and their associated productivity effects, see Giorgio Marrano, Haskel, and Wallis, 2007.

Another important source of MFP growth is the use of ICT. For instance, consider two firms that invest equally in ICT, but one employs it better to link its business processes so that sales, stock replenishment, customer service resources and marketing are all automatically linked with no need for manual intervention. Although they have made the same investment in ICT capital, the way it has been used means one firm enjoys a much greater boost in productivity. This also illustrates that MFP can be the result of the combination of capital and the skill level of the workforce or management.

Embodied technical change comes in the form of advances in the quality of capital or other inputs and so is captured when calculating the contribution of the inputs. An example of this is the rapid improvement in the quality of ICT over the last 20 years.

Other possible inputs, usually defined as intermediate inputs, that could be included in MFP analysis, are purchases of energy, materials and services. Although such inputs are not included in this analysis, they have been included in the EU KLEMS project (Van Ark, O'Mahony, Ypma, Groningen Growth and Development Centre, University of Groningen and University of Birmingham, 2007).

Methodology

A standard production function, as shown below in equation (1), can be used to derive equation (2) which states that growth in output is explained by the growth in capital, labour and the Solow residual, A(t) (Solow, 1957). αK and αL are the income shares of capital and labour and sum to one since we have assumed that there are constant returns to scale.

$$Y(t) = A(t)F(K(t),L(t)) \qquad (1)$$

$$\frac{\Delta Y(t)}{Y(t)} = \alpha K \frac{\Delta K(t)}{K(t)} + \alpha L \frac{\Delta L(t)}{L(t)} + A(t) \qquad (2)$$

Specifically, the residual is calculated using a rearrangement of the following equation:

$$\Delta \ln Y(t) = [1 - \bar{s}_L(t)] \Delta \ln K(t) + \bar{s}_L(t) \Delta \ln L(t) + \Delta \ln A(t) \quad (3)$$

where $\bar{s}_L$ is the average of the labour share of total income in the current and previous period, and the weight for capital is simply one minus the share for labour:

$$\bar{s}_L(t) = [s_L(t) + s_L(t-1)]/2 \quad (4)$$

The advantage of QALI over a standard labour input measure is that the contribution of skills is captured, at least partially, and is not attributed to a change in multi-factor productivity. In practice, some of the quality changes in labour and capital will still be present in the MFP term. Other factors that will be captured by the MFP term include adjustment costs, economies of scale, cyclical effects, the contribution of omitted inputs, inefficiencies and errors in the measurement of output.

The same technique can be used to decompose labour productivity growth into the contributions of physical capital deepening (capital income share multiplied by growth of physical capital per hour worked), labour composition (skills or the quality adjustment) and MFP growth as shown in equation (5):

$$\Delta \ln \left[\frac{Y(t)}{H(t)}\right] = [1 - \bar{s}_L(t)] \Delta \ln \left[\frac{K(t)}{H(t)}\right] + \bar{s}_L(t) [\Delta \ln L(t) - \Delta \ln H(t)] + \Delta \ln A(t) \quad (5)$$

where H(t) and L(t) represent standard and quality-adjusted hours, respectively. A standard aggregation of hours treats labour as a homogenous input, whereas quality-adjusted hours recognises the heterogeneity of labour and uses its profile in terms of education, experience, sex and industry to measure the added value it generates.

As mentioned previously, in practice, some of the quality change associated with labour, and also capital, will remain in the MFP term. Also, if the factor income shares are inaccurate approximations of the elasticities in the production function, then there will be errors in the estimation of the factor contributions and MFP.

Source data

Labour input
The data source for the labour input measure is the Labour Force Survey (LFS), a continuous household-based survey that covers approximately 53,000 households every quarter. It contains information on educational attainment, industry, sex and age. Under the assumption that different worker types have differing levels of

marginal productivity, labour hours are adjusted with regard to these characteristics. For detail on the quality adjustment process and why these characteristics have been chosen, see Holmwood, Richardson, Lau and Wallis (2005) or Goodridge (2006).

Capital services
Details on the calculation of capital services estimates can be found in Wallis (2005), with the latest available estimates described in Wallis (2007). It should be noted that capital services differs from the net capital stock measure in the National Accounts, the main difference being that it uses rentals to weight together assets rather than prices. The main asset types are buildings, plant and machinery, vehicles and intangibles, the largest component of the latter being software. Computers are separated out of plant and machinery and given shorter life-lengths and hence higher depreciation rates to ensure their productivity input is properly captured.

Output and factor income shares
The output measure used in this article is a chained volume measure (CVM) of GVA consistent with that published in *Blue Book* 2006, but does not contain any adjustments made as part of the National Accounts balancing process.

It should be noted that whole economy output growth can be modelled in terms of the capital and labour inputs. However, at industry level, some productivity changes may be the result of changes in expenditure on intermediate inputs. MFP analysis using intermediate inputs as factors of production will be part of the EU KLEMS project. For further details on this project, see ONS (2007). It will also be possible for ONS to use data on intermediates in MFP analysis when constant price input-output tables are produced as part of the modernised National Accounts system in time for *Blue Book* 2008.

Issues surrounding the calculation of labour's income share
In calculating the labour (and therefore the capital) shares of total income, the numerator is equal to compensation of employees from National Accounts plus the compensation of the self-employed. Since there is no National Accounts series for the labour income of the self-employed, this has to be estimated (the National Accounts series for self-employed earnings is 'mixed income', given its name because it includes both the returns to capital and labour in the self-employed sector). Therefore, two

choices were available, the first using data from the LFS on the average hourly wage for the employed and total self-employed hours in each relevant sector. These can be multiplied together to give estimates for the labour compensation of the self-employed. Alternatively, mixed income can be split using the relative proportions from compensation of employees and gross operating surplus by making the assumption that capital and labour generate the same returns in the self-employed sector as they do in the employed sector. In each case the denominator is total income, that is, the sum of compensation of employees, gross operating surplus and mixed income, taken from the Input-Output Supply and Use tables.

The initial choice was to estimate the labour income of the self-employed using microdata from the LFS. However, examination of the results showed that virtually all of mixed income was being allocated to labour, meaning capital generated zero returns, a nonsensical result. One possible explanation for this may be that self-employed income is under-reported for tax purposes and that much self-employed activity takes place in the hidden economy and is not picked up in official figures. The conclusion was also reached that there does not appear to be any good reason to believe that capital would generate a lower return in the self-employed sector than in the employed sector. Therefore the method of using the proportions from the employed sector was used.

However, for quality assurance, and to reassure the user, the analysis was also produced using the alternative methodology and in practice it makes little difference to the final results, since mixed income is such a small component of total income. The results of this exercise are presented in the Annex at the end of the article.

Results[1]
Figure 1 shows the decomposition of output growth into contributions from the factor inputs, capital and labour, and MFP growth. There are two sets of results with the first part based on a standard aggregation of hours and the second part based on quality-adjusted hours using information on workers characteristics. For the whole economy, using the unadjusted measure, MFP growth is estimated to have been 0.8 per cent per annum between 1997 and 2005.

Figure 1

Decomposition of annual average output growth, 1997 to 2005

(a) Unadjusted labour
Percentages

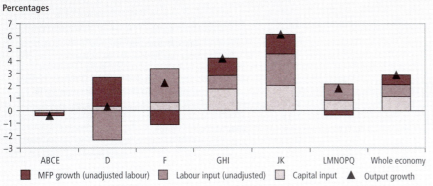

(b) Adjusted labour
Percentages

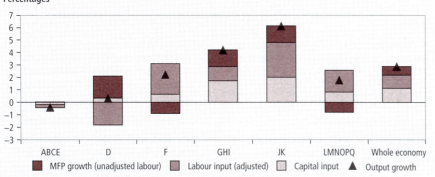

The following table provides a description of the sectors used in this analysis.

Table 1

Industry description

Industry	Industry description
ABCE	Agriculture, hunting, forestry, fishing, mining and quarrying, utilities
D	Manufacturing
F	Construction
GHI	Wholesale and retail trade, hotels and restaurants, transport storage and communication
JK	Financial intermediation, real estate, renting and business activities
LMNOPQ	Public administration and defence, education, health and social work, other social and personal services, and extra-territorial activities

Looking at individual sectors, the strongest growth has occurred in manufacturing (D), while there has also been growth in financial intermediation and business services (JK) and the combined sector of the distributive trades, hotels and restaurants, and transport and communication (GHI). MFP growth in the other sectors was negative over the period studied. For construction this was expected and is consistent with other studies over similar periods in both the UK and the US (Lau and Vaze, 2002). The result for LMNOPQ, which mainly comprises public

services, probably partially reflects the measurement of output in this sector in National Accounts which is still largely based on measures of inputs. For measures of public sector output based on outcomes that contain adjustments for quality, users should consult work produced by UKCeMGA at www.statistics.gov.uk/about/data/methodology/specific/publicsector/output/default.asp

When the adjustment is made for labour quality, MFP growth tends to reduce in most sectors, suggesting an improvement

in labour composition or skills over the period studied. However, this is not the case for all sectors, and the reverse is actually true in agriculture, mining and utilities (ABCE) and construction (F), reflecting a decline in the quality of labour in these sectors. Interestingly, this means the result for ABCE actually changes from negative to positive when quality-adjusted hours are used.

Figure 2 presents a similar analysis to the above, but this time on the decomposition of growth in labour productivity.

This chart shows that the contribution of labour composition for the whole economy was 0.1 percentage points a year, just 6.3 per cent of labour productivity growth, with capital deepening and MFP making much larger contributions. However, labour composition did make a larger contribution in manufacturing (D), making up 16.3 per cent of growth in labour productivity.

It can be seen that labour productivity tends to be lower in those industries contained in the service sector than manufacturing. This is often the nature of the sector, as in many cases the service offered is the product of labour itself, so it is often very labour-intensive with a much lesser role for capital than in the production sector. This is commonly referred to as 'Baumol's Disease' or the 'Baumol Effect'. The common example given by Baumol is that it takes the same number of musicians to play a Beethoven string quartet today as it did in the 19th century. This applies to various service sector industries – for instance it is hard to conceive how there could be significant productivity improvements among hairdressers. However, for many service sector industries, this appears to be changing with the development in ICT

Figure 2

Decomposition of annual average labour productivity growth, 1997 to 2005

Percentages

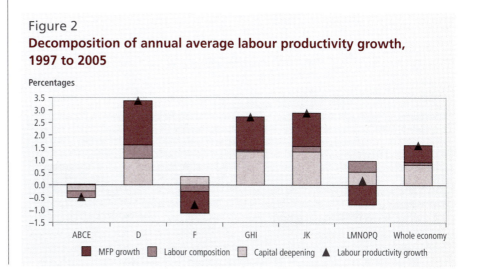

Table 2
Annual growth in labour composition

	ABCE	D	F	GHI	JK	LMNOPQ	Whole economy
1997	0.32	0.50	2.19	−0.88	2.31	−0.23	0.17
1998	−0.81	0.28	0.21	0.10	0.10	1.29	0.43
1999	0.35	1.43	0.65	0.45	0.06	0.39	0.38
2000	−0.99	1.30	−1.27	0.39	−0.70	0.85	0.19
2001	−0.76	0.67	0.85	0.45	0.06	−0.36	−0.11
2002	−2.62	0.84	−0.60	−0.45	0.73	0.78	−0.07
2003	2.74	0.70	−3.77	0.27	−0.21	0.34	−0.11
2004	−4.23	0.32	0.43	−0.46	0.59	0.99	0.08
2005	−2.72	0.56	−1.17	0.85	−0.17	0.78	0.27
Average	−0.97	0.73	−0.28	0.08	0.31	0.54	0.14

which has resulted in massive innovation to both products and processes in much of the service sector, particularly in finance and business services.

However, Figure 2 shows that although labour productivity growth in services is behind manufacturing, the share contributed by MFP growth is fairly similar, possibly reflecting the increased use of ICT in these industries.

Table 2 shows the growth in labour composition, by sector, over 1997 to 2005.

For the whole economy, labour composition grew on average by 0.1 per cent a year, with the highest growth occurring in manufacturing (D) and public and other services (LMNOPQ). However,

few conclusions can be drawn on the change in labour composition due to the short time period studied. The labour measure is based on hours worked, which is a far more cyclical measure than workers or jobs, with firms responding to changing demand conditions by increasing or reducing hours in the short-term, rather than hiring or dismissing workers. Therefore, if such changes affect different worker types differently, there will be a change in labour composition. In general it would be expected that labour composition would rise during a slump when the less skilled and experienced workers are the first to be laid off, and fall during a boom when less productive workers are drawn back into the labour market due to

increased demand. Therefore, the seemingly slow growth in labour composition since 1997 may reflect the strength of the UK economy over this period.

As a final piece of analysis, the period studied has been split into two separate parts, before and after 2000, the main reason being the difference in capital investment. Before 2000, firms made larger, possibly unnecessarily large, investments in ICT in attempts to avert the 'millennium bug'. This, in turn, often resulted in much lower investment just after 2000 as capital had already recently been replaced. This is reflected in the capital services growth estimates presented in Wallis (2007). A decomposition of output growth for the two periods is presented in **Figure 3** and **Figure 4**.

The results show that the contribution of capital in the latter period was lower, although so was growth in output. In terms of percentages, the contribution of capital to growth in output was 41.9 per cent in 1997 to 2000 compared with 36.5 per cent in 2001 to 2005. Results for the other sectors tell a similar story. The difference is particularly stark in manufacturing where, in the latter period, the contribution of capital was actually zero, although output did decline over the period. The same is true of construction, where the contribution of capital fell from 55.4 per cent of output growth to 21.4 per cent between the two periods.

Looking specifically at MFP growth, the latter period shows a significant decline in agriculture, mining and utilities but strong improvement in manufacturing and construction.

Figure 5 decomposes labour productivity growth for each period.

The results show that the decline in labour productivity growth between the two periods is mainly due to a fall in labour composition, again reflecting the view that with employment at historically high levels, less productive workers are being drawn into the workforce due to favourable demand conditions, although this does vary between sectors. The contributions of physical capital deepening and MFP growth are broadly similar between the two periods, although again there is some variation in individual industries.

This article has presented analysis of MFP growth using the quality-adjusted input measures developed by ONS, QALI and VICS, meaning growth in MFP is more accurately estimated. However, the short time period studied is not ideal for analysis of this sort, with growth of MFP being volatile in the short-run, and the estimates will improve as the series is lengthened.

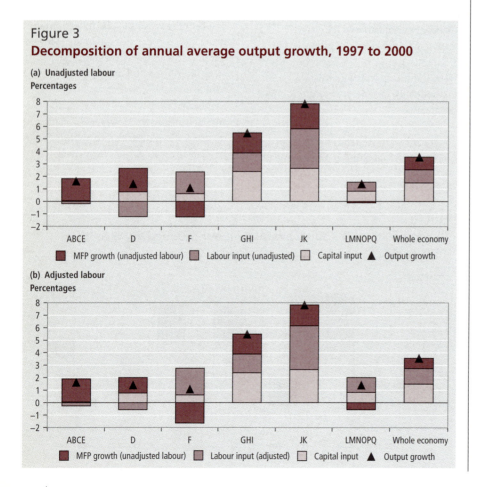

Figure 3
Decomposition of annual average output growth, 1997 to 2000

(a) Unadjusted labour
Percentages

MFP growth (unadjusted labour) ■ Labour input (unadjusted) □ Capital input ▲ Output growth

(b) Adjusted labour
Percentages

MFP growth (unadjusted labour) ■ Labour input (adjusted) □ Capital input ▲ Output growth

Figure 4
Decomposition of annual average output growth, 2001 to 2005

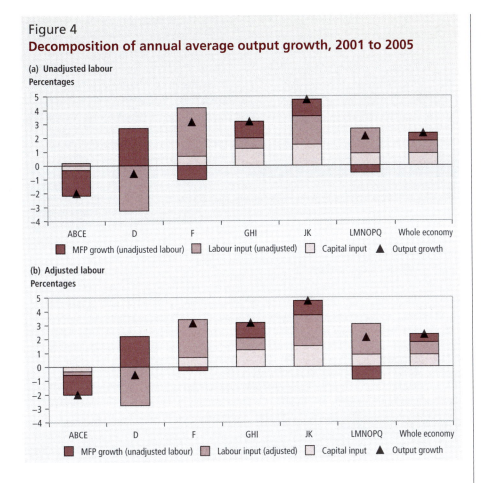

(a) Unadjusted labour
Percentages

■ MFP growth (unadjusted labour)   ■ Labour input (unadjusted)   ☐ Capital input   ▲ Output growth

(b) Adjusted labour
Percentages

■ MFP growth (unadjusted labour)   ■ Labour input (adjusted)   ☐ Capital input   ▲ Output growth

Figure 5
Decomposition of annual average labour productivity growth

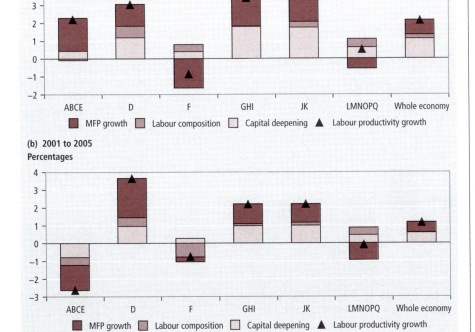

(a) 1997 to 2000
Percentages

■ MFP growth   ■ Labour composition   ☐ Capital deepening   ▲ Labour productivity growth

(b) 2001 to 2005
Percentages

■ MFP growth   ■ Labour composition   ☐ Capital deepening   ▲ Labour productivity growth

Unfortunately, it is not possible to extend the series further back due to breaks in the qualification variable on which QALI is partially based. In terms of the results, the UK is still not experiencing a surge in productivity growth as seen in other countries, possibly driven by increased investment in ICT, most notably the US. This suggests that ICT in the UK may not be employed as effectively, possibly as a result of the relatively low skill base of the UK labour force or less effective organisational structure and management. Thus policy may be needed to assist the five drivers of productivity, particularly skills and investment.

Note

1   All results contained in this article are in the form of bar charts. For actual data presented in greater detail, please see www.statistics.gov.uk/cci/searches.asp?term=mfp

ACKNOWLEGEMENTS

The author is grateful for comments and advice from Jonathan Haskel, Mauro Giorgio Marrano, Sally Srinivasan and Gavin Wallis.

CONTACT

 elmr@ons.gsi.gov.uk

REFERENCES

Bell V, Burriel-Llombart P and Jones J (2005) 'A quality-adjusted labour input series for the United Kingdom (1975–2002)', Bank of England Working Paper No. 280.

Camus D and Lau E (2006) 'Productivity Measures and analysis: ONS Strategy and work programme', *Economic Trends* 632 pp 14–21 and at www.statistics.gov.uk/cci/article.asp?id=1603

Giorgio Marrano M, Haskel J and Wallis G (2007) 'What Happened to the Knowledge Economy? ICT, Intangible Investment and Britain's Productivity Record Revisited', *Queen Mary College Working Article 603.*

Goodridge P (2006) 'Experimental quality-adjusted labour input measure – 1996 to 2005', *Economic Trends* 637 pp 46–56 and at www.statistics.gov.uk/cci/article.asp?id=1693

Holmwood R, Lau E, Richardson C and Wallis G (2005) 'An experimental quality-adjusted labour input measure', *Economic Trends* 624 pp 30–41 and at www.statistics.gov.uk/cci/article.asp?id=1298

Lau E (2002) 'Productivity Measures: ONS strategy', *Economic Trends* 581, pp 20–5 and at
www.statistics.gov.uk/cci/article.asp?id=145

Lau E and Vaze P (2002) 'Accounting growth: capital, skills and output' at
www.statistics.gov.uk/cci/nscl.asp?id=8311

Office for National Statistics (2007) *The ONS Productivity Handbook: A Statistical Overview and Guide* at
www.statistics.gov.uk/about/data/guides/productivity/default.asp

Solow R (1957) 'Technical change and the Aggregate Production Function', *Review of Economics and Statistics* Vol 39 pp 312–20.

Van Ark B, O'Mahony M, Ypma G, Groningen Growth and Development Centre, University of Groningen, University of Birmingham (2007) 'The EU KLEMS Productivity Report' at
www.euklems.com/data/eu_klems_productivity_report.pdf

Wallis G (2005) 'Estimates of the volume of capital services', *Economic Trends* 624 pp 42–51 and at
www.statistics.gov.uk/cci/article.asp?id=1297

Wallis G (2007) 'Volume of capital services: estimates for 1950 to 2005', *Economic & Labour Market Review* 1(7) pp 39–47 and at
www.statistics.gov.uk/cci/article.asp?id=1827

ANNEX

Presented below is the decomposition of output growth, and also labour productivity, calculated by using the LFS to approximate self-employed labour income and calculate the factor income shares.

Figure A1
Decomposition of annual average output growth, alternative methodology, 1997 to 2005

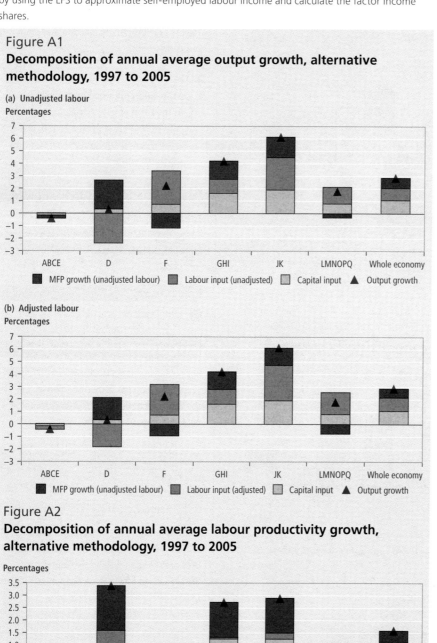

(a) Unadjusted labour
Percentages

(b) Adjusted labour
Percentages

Figure A2
Decomposition of annual average labour productivity growth, alternative methodology, 1997 to 2005

Percentages

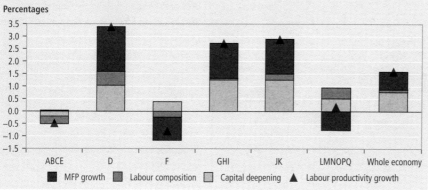

FEATURE

Gavin Wallis
HM Treasury

Volume of capital services: estimates for 1950 to 2005

SUMMARY

Capital services are the measure of capital input that is suitable for analysing and modelling productivity. This article presents experimental estimates of the volume of capital services for the UK as a whole, for the market sector, by five asset types and also by detailed industry. The key features of the estimates include the strong growth in capital services from computers and also much stronger growth in the services industries than in the production industries over recent years. The estimates presented here are being used by the Office for National Statistics to produce official multi-factor productivity estimates for the UK.

Capital and labour are key factors of production, both contributing to the output of the economy. There is considerable interest in measuring these two inputs accurately for use in productivity and other types of economic analysis. However, defining capital and measuring its contribution to production has been a contentious issue for both economists and statisticians for many years. Early work in this area includes Jorgenson (1963), the seminal paper on growth accounting by Jorgenson and Griliches (1967), Hall and Jorgenson (1967) on the cost of capital, and the work of Hulten and Wykoff (1981a, 1981b) on the estimation of depreciation rates. More recently there has been a degree of international agreement about the conceptual issues concerning the stocks and flows of capital. The Organisation for Economic Co-operation and Development (OECD) published a manual in 2001 (OECD, 2001) covering the measurement of capital stocks and providing practical guidelines for estimation. Recent work by Oulton and Srinivasan (2003) has also proposed an integrated framework for measuring capital stocks, capital services and depreciation.

Capital services estimates weight together the growth of the net stock of assets using weights that reflect the relative productivity of the different assets that make up the capital stock. This is in contrast to the capital stock estimates in the UK National Accounts, which use asset prices as weights. The capital stock estimates in the National Accounts are therefore wealth estimates of the capital stock while capital services are a flow measure that reflects the input of capital into production. Capital services are the measure of capital input that is suitable for analysing and modelling productivity. This is because, by definition, a capital asset generates a stream of services that spans more than one accounting period. In essence, capital services are a measure of the actual contribution of the capital stock of assets to the production process in a given year.

There is much interest in how capital stocks impact on growth empirically and the link between productivity growth and capital has been discussed with particular reference to the recent large investments in assets related to the new economy, such as computers and other forms of information and communication technology. Capital services provide a more suitable measure for this purpose than the existing gross and net capital stock measures available in the UK National Accounts because they recognise both the short life length of these assets and the rapid price falls observed in such high-technology goods. As shown by Oulton and Srinivasan (2003), UK capital stock measures (and capital services measures) are sensitive to the treatment of assets with a short life length, such as computers. For this reason, the capital services estimates presented here treat computers as a separate asset and subsequently provide a better measure of the flow of input from the capital stock into production.

This article is an update to Wallis (2005) and presents capital services estimates up to 2005 and revised estimates for previous years. In addition, a new series is also included: market sector capital services.

The definition of market sector is consistent with that used in Marks (2007) and so the capital services estimates could be used together with the Office for National Statistics (ONS) market sector output data in productivity analysis of the market sector. For example, the market sector net stock data underlying the capital services estimates in this article were used in the growth accounting analysis in Giorgio Marrano, Haskel, and Wallis (2007).

An accompanying article in this edition of *Economic & Labour Market Review* (Goodridge, 2007) describes a published set of official multifactor productivity estimates for the UK. The estimates use the capital services data described in this article as the capital input in the multi-factor productivity analysis alongside the quality-adjusted labour input (QALI) measure described in Goodridge (2006).

Estimation methodology

The methodology used to estimate capital services is described in detail in Wallis (2005) and in *The ONS Productivity Handbook* (ONS, 2007) and so will not be repeated here.

Data

The data used to estimate capital services are the same as those underpinning the UK National Accounts capital stock estimates and are consistent with *Blue Book* 2006. The data set consists of a long time series of constant price investment data, classified by industry, life length means and price deflators.

Maintaining consistency with *Blue Book* 2006 means that the capital services estimates presented here are ideal for multi-factor productivity work, as this means they are consistent with the output measures (gross value added – GVA) in the UK National Accounts.

The asset breakdown of the investment series is buildings, plant and machinery, vehicles and intangibles. In order to treat computers as a separate asset, computer investment has to be separated from investment in plant and machinery and the associated price deflators have to be adjusted to account for this. It should be noted that, although an appropriate life length is used for computers in the National Accounts (currently assumed to be five years), the capital stock estimates do not separately deflate computers, and so they are not fully treated as a separate asset in the National Accounts.

Ideally, software would also be treated as a separate asset. This is not done here

as current data sources make this difficult. Software is not identified as a separate asset in the National Accounts and a suitable software deflator has yet to be incorporated into the National Accounts. In the existing National Accounts, investment data for purchased software is included in plant and machinery, while software developed in-house, called own-account software, is included in intangibles. The overall results presented here will not be affected, as long as the price of purchased software moves in line with the price of plant and machinery and the price of own-account software moves in line the with the price of intangibles. In practice, and based on the US software deflator, it is likely that the price of software is falling in relative terms meaning the estimated growth rate of capital services has a slight downwards bias.

Following the revisions to software investment described in Chamberlin, Clayton and Farooqui (2007), it should be possible to treat software as a separate asset when estimating capital services.

For all assets, investment is taken as the starting stock for the first year in which the investment series is available. For buildings, plant and machinery, vehicles, and intangibles, the investment series starts well before 1950 (as early as 1828 for some of the buildings series) and so any initial conditions problems can be ignored. For computers, sensitivity analysis showed that, due to these assets depreciating quickly, the capital services estimates were insensitive to different methods for calculating the starting stock.

Treatment of computers as a separate asset

Due to the relative price of computers falling rapidly, and their economic lives being much shorter than those of most other types of plant and machinery, the treatment of computers as a separate asset is now standard in capital stock models. The methodology used to calculate capital services will give more weight to assets for which the rental price is high in relation to the asset price, which is the case for computers. As such, computers are treated as a separate asset here.

In order to treat computers as a separate asset, a time series of constant price investment data is needed, together with an appropriate life length mean and a price deflator. This is not currently available from the UK National Accounts. The basis for estimating computer investment here is the current price computer investment available in the most recent supply-use

analysis. In this case, the supply-use analysis is consistent with *Blue Book* 2006. Current price computer investment can be obtained from Table 6 of the supply-use tables (product 69) and is currently available at the 57-industry level. As the most recent supply-use tables only cover the period 1992 to 2005, a previous supply-use table for 1984 was used in order to get a series covering the period 1984 to 2005, with the interim years being interpolated.

As noted above, a life length mean for computers is already used in the UK National Accounts capital stock estimation and so this same life length mean is used here, with a double-declining balance method used to give the depreciation rate (see Wallis, 2005).

The computers producer price index (PPI) is used as the computer deflator (ONS code PQEK), which is available from 1986. The computer deflator for 1984 and 1985 has been estimated by projecting backwards the 1986 to 1987 growth rate of this PPI. An alternative is to use the growth in the US computer deflator for these two years. This alternative has an insignificant effect on the results presented here. Using the US deflator for the entire period instead of the UK one also has an insignificant impact on the estimates presented here. Combining the current price computer investment, obtained using the supply-use tables, and the computer deflator, constant price computers investment can be generated as required for estimating capital services.

Plant and machinery investment, as well as the associated plant and machinery PPIs, all have to be adjusted to take account of the treatment of computers as a separate asset. The method has been to constrain total investment, in both current price and constant price to UK National Accounts totals to maintain consistency with the National Accounts capital stock estimates. This means that the plant and machinery PPIs have to be adjusted to remove the effect of computer prices. As computers are an asset for which prices have been falling rapidly, this has a positive effect on asset price growth for plant and machinery.

Capital services estimates

This section presents capital services estimates for the whole economy, for the market sector, by five asset types and also by industry. A 57-industry breakdown, consistent with the most recent supply-use analysis, is presented together with a six-industry breakdown consistent with the industry breakdown at which the ONS QALI measure is published (Goodridge, 2006).

In most cases estimates are available for the period 1950 to 2005. However, due to space limitations, not all available data are presented here. A full set of results including downloadable data tables is available from www.statistics.gov.uk/statbase/product.asp?vlnk=14205

Capital services in the UK

Figure 1 shows the annual growth in capital services for the UK over the period 1950 to 2005. It can be seen that there is strong and sustained growth up to the early 1970s. This early period suffers from one notable measurement issue – quantifying the one-off loss of capital associated with the Second World War. The official estimates of this loss are provided by Dean (1964). The 1970s saw more modest capital services growth, falling in most years up until the early 1980s. This period coincides with UK recessions in 1973 to 1975 and 1979 to 1982, following the oil shocks in 1973 and 1979. During this period, net stock grew very slowly, with a large negative impact from premature scrapping of capital assets. The series reaches its lowest point in 1981, with annual growth of just 1 per cent.

After 1981, capital services growth began to increase, reaching a local peak of over 4 per cent in 1989. It then fell rapidly in the early 1990s, as a result of the recession in the UK. In the late 1990s and in more recent years, capital services have shown very strong growth, peaking in 1998 at 7 per cent. As will be seen later, this strong growth is driven by high levels of investment in computers and the associated growth in capital services from this asset. Average growth for the period 1950 to 2005 was 3.3 per cent, while growth in the last ten years averaged 4.5 per cent.

Also shown in Figure 1 is the annual growth in the wealth measures of net stock from the UK National Accounts. The National Accounts series is the growth in total net stock excluding dwellings (net stock excluding dwellings is calculated as ONS code GUCJ minus ONS code EXJF). The close fit of the two series is to be expected as they are both based on the same raw data set, consisting of long time series of capital formation data, deflators and life length means (assumed life lengths of assets). The differences in the two series are due to the separate deflation of computers, the use of geometric rather than arithmetic depreciation and the weighting of net asset growth by profit shares rather than in asset value terms as in the National Accounts. Average growth over the period 1950 to 2005 is slightly less for the National

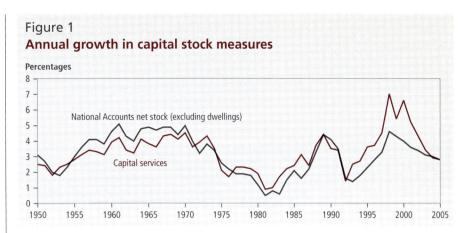

Figure 1

Annual growth in capital stock measures

Percentages

National Accounts net stock (excluding dwellings)

Capital services

Accounts net stock (3.1 per cent) than for capital services (3.3 per cent).

The larger divergence in the series, starting in the late 1990s, is due to the separate deflation of computers in the capital services estimates, a method not currently used for estimating the National Accounts capital stock, and also the fact that capital services account for the productivity contribution of computers better than a capital stock estimate does. The period after 1990 was one of fast-growing investment in computers while their price fell rapidly. This combination makes the share of computers in the whole economy capital services estimates grow over time (see Figure 7) and makes capital services grow more rapidly.

An interesting way to look at the divergence of the National Accounts wealth-based measures of capital stock and capital services is as volume indices. **Figure 2** shows that there is a clear divergence between the volume of capital

services and the volume of capital stock after 1980, especially after 1990. This divergence is being driven by the shift towards short-lived and more productive assets, such as computers, for which the flow of capital services is high. The standard capital stock measure does not adequately capture this shift and so understates growth in the productive input of capital in the UK economy, especially after 1990.

Revisions since previous release

Revisions to capital services estimates since Wallis (2005) are minimal and are just due to revisions to the underlying constant price investment series. A full revisions analysis is not shown here due to the large number of series being presented. However, **Figure 3** shows the new estimates of whole-economy capital services growth against the previously published estimates. It can be seen that the revisions are small in magnitude and are to post-1985 estimates only.

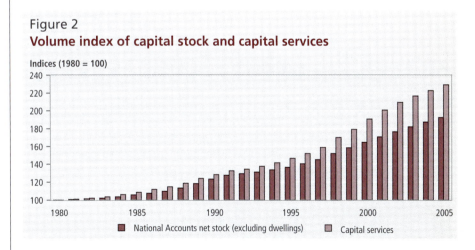

Figure 2

Volume index of capital stock and capital services

Indices (1980 = 100)

■ National Accounts net stock (excluding dwellings)   ■ Capital services

Figure 3
Annual growth in capital services: new and previous estimates

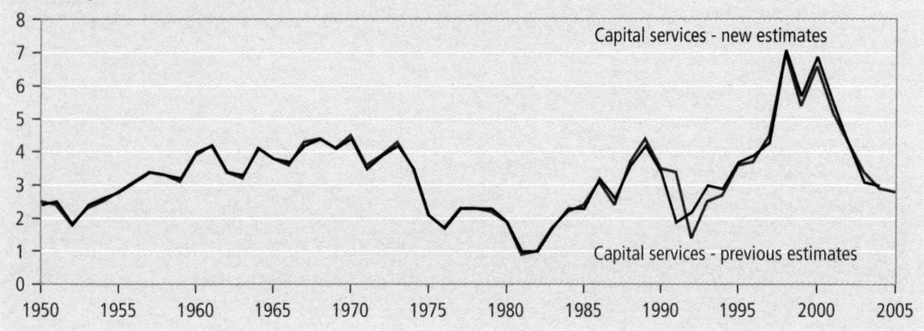

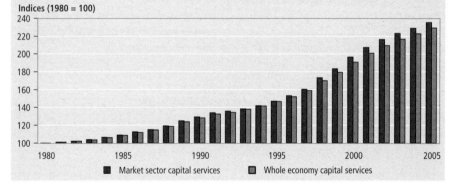

Percentages

Market sector capital services

Productivity and other macroeconomic analysis often focuses on the market sector rather than the whole economy. This is especially true when making international comparisons of productivity, undertaking growth accounting analysis, or when estimating and analysing business cycles. **Figure 4** shows the volume of market sector capital services relative to the whole economy. The market sector here is consistent with the definition of the National Accounts market sector output measure, making it suitable for use in market sector growth accounting analysis.

It is clear that market sector capital services have been growing faster than for the whole economy. The main reason behind this divergence is that the market sector has been investing more heavily in computers than government.

Capital services by asset type

Figure 5 shows annual growth in capital services by asset type. Computers are not shown, as capital services from computers grew much faster than other assets, especially in the late 1990s, and their inclusion would hide much of the variation in the other assets. Interesting points to

note from Figure 5 are:

- the 1950s and 1960s saw strong and relatively stable growth in capital services for all assets
- growth in capital services from buildings is relatively stable over the period in comparison with the growth in capital services for other asset types
- for all assets there is a downturn in capital services growth in the mid-1970s, driven by a fall in the net stock in many industries over this period
- capital services growth rates are subdued for all assets during the recession in the early 1990s
- negative capital services growth only occurs for vehicles and intangibles and the periods of sustained negative capital services growth occur during the period following the first oil shock and the recession in the 1990s

Figure 6 shows the volume of capital services from computers relative to the volume of whole economy capital services. The volume index of the former increases to nearly 3,000 in 2005 from 100 in 1987, while the volume index of whole economy capital services (all assets) increases to just 200 by 2005. This explains the divergence seen in Figure 2 between the wealth-based National Accounts measures of net stock and capital services. The reason that the growth in capital services from computers is not driving up whole economy (all assets) capital services more is that computers still only account for a 10 per cent share of profits (see Figure 7).

Table 1 summarises capital services growth by asset type for selected periods. The periods chosen are cyclical peak-to-peak and the table shows average annual growth over these periods. Interesting points to note from Table 1 are:

- average annual growth in capital services from buildings is similar in all time periods
- capital services from plant and machinery has been weaker in more recent cycles, perhaps reflecting the move towards computers and away from traditional plant and machinery and also a shift in the economy towards services and away from manufacturing
- capital services growth from vehicles has been relatively weak in all except the period 2000 to 2005: this is due to weak capital stock growth and possibly reflects the impact of high oil prices and the two oil shocks

Figure 4
Volume index of whole economy and market sector capital services

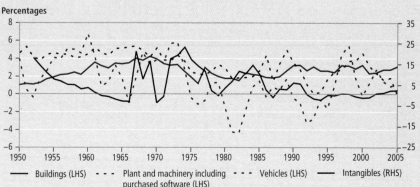

Indices (1980 = 100)

Figure 5
Annual growth in capital services: by asset type

Percentages

Figure 6
Volume index of whole economy and computers capital services

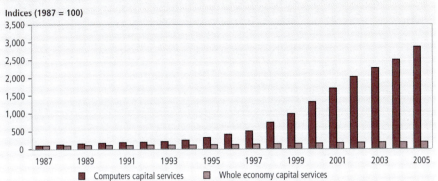

Indices (1987 = 100)

Legend: ■ Computers capital services   ▨ Whole economy capital services

Table 1
Average annual growth rates of capital services: by asset type

Percentages

	1973–79	1979–90	1990–2000	2000–05
Buildings	2.2	2.1	2.9	2.7
Plant and machinery	2.8	2.8	2.3	1.8
Vehicles	0.5	− 0.7	0.3	1.5
Intangibles	11.6	6.7	0.4	1.5
Computers	n/a	n/a	23.3	16.9

- capital services from intangibles grew very rapidly in the period 1973 to 1979, reflecting exploration of North Sea oil
- capital services growth from computers was stronger in the run-up to the millennium than it has been since, possibly reflecting overinvestment in the earlier period in response to the feared 'millennium bug'

Capital services by industry

Capital services estimates have been produced at both 57-industry and six-industry levels. The 57-industry breakdown is consistent with the most recent supply-use analysis. The six-industry breakdown coincides with that at which the ONS QALI measure is published (Goodridge, 2006) and are the capital services estimates used in the multi-factor productivity analysis presented in the accompanying article in this edition of *Economic & Labour Market Review*.

Table 2 shows growth in capital services by industry for selected periods. As in Table 1, the periods chosen are cyclical peak-to-peak and the table shows average annual growth over these periods. Also included are estimates for aggregate production industries and aggregate services industries as well as medians and 25th and 75th percentiles.

Interesting points to note from Table 2 are:

- in all periods, the average annual growth rate of capital services is higher for aggregate services, industries than for aggregate production industries
- production industries saw their strongest growth in capital services in the period 1973 to 1979, and this was followed by much weaker growth in latter periods: as low as 0.1 per cent in the period 2000 to 2005
- average annual growth of capital services in the services industries has been stronger in each period, rising from 2.5 per cent in the period 1973 to 1979 to 5.7 per cent in the period 2000 to 2005
- services industries only saw positive average annual growth in capital services in the periods 1990 to 2000 and 2000 to 2005, while in all periods some production industries saw negative average annual growth in capital services
- the medians and 25th and 75th percentiles show that average annual growth is much more dispersed in the production industries than in the services industries; high-tech production industries, such as medical and precision instruments, show

continued strong capital services growth while many other production industries experienced falling capital services
- over the two most recent periods, auxiliary financial services saw the strongest growth in capital services, while forestry saw the largest fall in capital services, this reflecting the changing nature of the UK economy, with a very strong financial sector and a weaker manufacturing and agricultural sector
- industries that are large users of computers, such as computer services and research and development, showed the strongest average annual growth in capital services

Also included in Table 2 are average annual growth rates of GVA for the production and services industries. It is interesting to note that the increase in capital services growth in the services industries over time was matched by stronger growth in services industry GVA, as might be expected, and also that growth in capital services was faster than growth in GVA in all periods. In contrast, production industry GVA growth averaged 1.3 per cent in the first three periods then declined to negative average annual growth in the latest period. In all but the period 1979 to 1990, capital services in the production industries grew more quickly than GVA.

Table 3 shows annual growth in the volume of capital services for six industries. The data are much less informative than in Table 2 as they hide much of the variation across lower levels of industry disaggregation. However, these are the estimates used in ONS multi-factor productivity work, as QALI is currently only available at this industry breakdown.

The results reinforce the discussion above with regard to production versus services industries. The first three industries cover production and it is clear that capital services growth is lower than that for the last three industries, which cover services.

Unsurprisingly, industry 5 – financial intermediation, real estate, renting and business activities – shows the fastest growth in capital services over the period. This strong capital services growth will be due to strong growth in investment, with computer investment making up a significant proportion of total investment for this industry.

Table 2
Average annual growth rates in capital services: by industry

Percentages

Industry	1973–79	1979–90	1990–2000	2000–05
Production industries				
Agriculture	1.1	–0.4	2.9	–2.1
Forestry	0.9	4.9	–1.9	–2.4
Fishing	1.6	–6.7	–6.5	–5.6
Coal extraction	3.2	0.2	–4.4	–4.3
Oil and gas extraction	27.7	5.5	0.7	–2.2
Other mining and quarrying	0.4	–1.7	–2.0	–0.8
Food products and beverages	2.9	1.7	2.0	0.8
Tobacco products	1.9	–0.7	2.2	–1.4
Textiles	–0.2	–1.8	–0.1	–2.4
Wearing apparel and fur products	0.6	–0.8	0.5	–2.9
Leather goods and footwear	n/a	n/a	2.7	–1.8
Wood and wood products	2.5	–1.6	0.6	1.5
Pulp, paper and paper products	8.2	18.9	12.8	2.0
Printing and publishing	3.0	2.2	2.3	1.6
Coke, refined petroleum and nuclear fuel	–0.6	2.5	0.3	–2.0
Chemicals and chemical products	2.3	0.9	3.3	–0.5
Rubber and plastic products	2.6	2.3	4.4	–0.7
Other non-metallic mineral products	5.8	5.2	1.6	0.8
Basic metals	1.5	–3.3	–1.0	–1.7
Metal products	1.9	–0.2	2.4	1.8
Machinery and equipment	3.0	0.3	1.5	0.3
Office machinery and computers	4.5	7.6	8.6	–0.4
Electrical machinery	1.9	–1.3	1.6	–1.8
Radio, TV and communication equipment	8.2	15.5	7.9	–5.5
Medical and precision instruments	3.7	2.8	11.6	4.4
Motor vehicles	2.8	2.1	3.2	0.2
Other transport equipment	0.4	1.1	0.1	5.7
Other manufacturing	2.9	1.7	5.0	2.3
Recycling	9.0	9.3	0.9	7.0
Electricity and gas	–0.3	–0.3	0.1	0.8
Water	–0.4	2.7	9.3	7.7
Construction	1.8	0.8	2.4	7.2
All production industries	2.4	1.0	1.8	0.1
Median	2.3	1.1	1.8	–0.4
25th percentile	1.0	–0.5	0.3	–2.0
75th percentile	3.1	2.7	3.2	1.7
Production industries GVA	1.3	1.3	1.3	–1.0
Services industries				
Motor vehicle distribution and repairs, fuel	8.3	14.9	7.7	10.1
Wholesale distribution	4.6	4.2	6.2	3.7
Retail distribution	4.6	4.2	6.1	7.2
Hotels and restaurants	4.1	4.8	6.2	5.4
Land transport and transport via pipelines	1.1	–0.4	0.9	2.0
Water transport	–4.3	–8.3	6.8	2.1
Air transport	2.9	–3.6	14.1	8.5
Ancillary transport services	1.8	2.8	7.5	12.2
Post and tele-communications	2.3	1.5	8.5	3.5
Financial intermediation	4.5	11.7	4.3	3.4
Insurance and pension funds	9.1	11.0	4.1	1.6
Auxiliary financial services	n/a	n/a	16.9	25.2
Real estate activities	3.2	5.7	4.4	9.5
Renting of machinery etc	16.8	9.7	10.6	7.2
Computer services	8.3	33.8	25.9	20.0
Research and development	8.3	35.7	22.0	12.0
Other business services	11.2	18.1	12.5	6.3
Public administration and defence	1.4	2.3	2.5	3.8
Education	1.7	0.7	2.1	5.3
Health and social work	5.4	4.6	3.9	4.5
Sewage and sanitary services	5.4	2.3	3.0	5.2
Membership organisations	8.4	14.1	5.9	6.7
Recreational services	4.9	6.1	6.5	6.1
Other services activities	8.4	15.1	5.7	9.7
All services industries	2.5	3.7	5.6	5.7
Median	4.6	4.8	6.2	6.2
25th percentile	2.6	2.3	4.2	3.7
75th percentile	8.3	12.9	9.0	9.5
Services industries GVA	1.8	2.5	3.2	3.2

Table 3

Annual growth in the volume of capital services: by aggregate industries

Percentages

Industry	1997	1998	1999	2000	2001	2002	2003	2004	2005
1 Agriculture, hunting, forestry, fishing, mining and quarrying, utilities	0.5	0.7	–0.8	–0.1	–0.2	0.2	–0.6	–0.2	–1.5
2 Manufacturing	3.3	4.0	2.4	2.0	1.5	–0.2	0.2	–1.2	0.1
3 Construction	5.4	4.4	6.7	6.6	2.9	12.6	7.4	10.6	2.3
4 Wholesale and retail trade, hotels and restaurants, transport storage and communication	8.9	10.2	8.2	10.5	9.9	7.3	4.1	1.9	2.6
5 Financial intermediation, real estate, renting and business activities	4.4	18.4	14.2	15.1	10.0	8.5	6.2	7.2	7.7
6 Public administration and defence, education, health and social work, other social and personal services, and extra-territorial activities	3.0	3.6	4.5	4.9	4.7	4.9	5.1	5.4	3.5

Profit shares

The weight of each asset or industry in calculating whole economy capital services is the share of gross operating surplus attributable to each asset or to each industry. These are usually referred to as profit shares. The time profile of the profit shares by asset over the period 1950 to 2005 is shown in **Figure 7**.

Figure 7 shows that the composition of profit shares has changed since the 1950s. The share of buildings has generally fallen, while that of vehicles has remained fairly constant. The share of plant and machinery has been more variable, increasing in the

1960s and 1970s, falling considerably during the period 1990 to 1994, before returning to a level similar to the 1950s by 2000 to 2005. Most interesting is the rise in the profit share of computers. From zero in 1980 to 1984 (in which period computers are not separately identified from plant and machinery), the profit share of computers has increased each period, culminating in a share of 10 per cent in the period 2000 to 2005.

Table 4 shows profit shares by industry for selected years. Those shown are 1973, 1979, 1990, 2000 and 2005, for ease of comparison with the capital services growth estimates presented in Table 2.

Interesting points to note from Table 4 are:

- the profit share of production industries falls from 54 per cent in 1973 to 33 per cent in 2005
- in contrast, the profit share of services industries increases from 46 per cent in 1973 to 67 per cent in 2005, reflecting the shift in the UK economy from manufacturing to services
- in 1973 electricity and gas is the industry with the largest profit share, while in 2005 it is public administration and defence
- industries with the largest increases in profit share include real estate activities, recreational services and other business services (all services industries)
- industries with the largest falls in profit share include electricity and gas, basic metals and agriculture (all production industries).

Conclusion

This article presented experimental estimates of the capital services growth for the UK as a whole, for the market sector, by five asset types and also by detailed industry. The key features of the estimates include the strong growth in capital services from computers and also much stronger growth in the services industries than in the production industries over recent years. There has also been a clear shift in the profit share from other assets to computers and also from production industries to services industries.

The divergence between the volume of capital services and the volume of capital stock after 1980, especially after 1990, has also been highlighted. This divergence is being driven by the shift towards short-lived and more productive assets, such as computers, for which the flow of capital services is high. It is important to recognise this divergence when considering UK productivity. Capital services and not capital stock should be used when conducting productivity analysis.

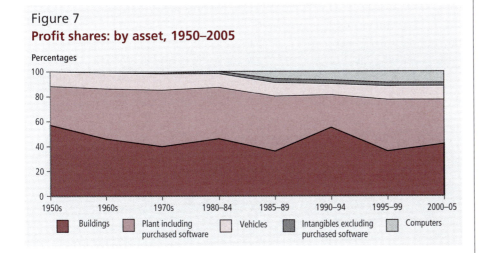

Figure 7

Profit shares: by asset, 1950–2005

Percentages

Legend: Buildings | Plant including purchased software | Vehicles | Intangibles excluding purchased software | Computers

Table 4
Profit shares: by industry

					Percentages
Industry	1973	1979	1990	2000	2005
Production industries					
Agriculture	3.9	4.3	3.2	3.3	2.2
Forestry	0.0	0.0	0.1	0.1	0.1
Fishing	0.3	0.1	0.1	0.0	0.0
Coal extraction	1.5	1.6	1.6	0.7	0.6
Oil and gas extraction	0.8	3.8	5.8	5.9	4.7
Other mining and quarrying	1.4	1.3	0.7	0.4	0.4
Food products and beverages	3.6	3.4	2.8	2.6	2.4
Tobacco products	0.3	0.2	0.1	0.1	0.1
Textiles	2.0	1.7	0.7	0.5	0.4
Wearing apparel and fur products	0.5	0.4	0.3	0.2	0.2
Leather goods and footwear	0.0	0.0	0.0	0.1	0.0
Wood and wood products	0.5	0.5	0.3	0.3	0.2
Pulp, paper and paper products	0.0	0.1	0.3	0.6	0.3
Printing and publishing	2.1	2.3	2.0	1.5	1.2
Coke, refined petroleum and nuclear fuel	1.5	1.5	1.3	1.2	1.0
Chemicals and chemical products	5.7	5.8	3.3	3.1	2.8
Rubber and plastic products	1.1	1.1	0.8	0.9	0.7
Other non-metallic mineral products	0.5	0.7	0.8	0.7	0.6
Basic metals	3.4	3.4	1.4	1.0	0.9
Metal products	1.6	1.5	1.0	0.9	0.7
Machinery and equipment	2.7	2.9	2.0	1.1	0.9
Office machinery and computers	0.2	0.2	0.2	0.3	0.2
Electrical machinery	1.6	1.9	0.8	0.5	0.3
Radio, TV and communication equipment	0.0	0.4	0.7	0.8	0.5
Medical and precision instruments	0.2	0.3	0.2	0.2	0.2
Motor vehicles	2.5	2.4	1.6	1.9	1.8
Other transport equipment	0.9	0.9	0.7	0.8	0.8
Other manufacturing	0.3	0.3	0.3	0.4	0.3
Recycling	0.0	0.1	0.1	0.1	0.1
Electricity and gas	12.6	9.4	6.9	6.6	5.0
Water	0.3	0.2	0.7	1.3	1.6
Construction	2.1	2.5	1.4	1.4	1.8
All production industries	54.0	55.2	42.6	39.4	32.9
Services industries					
Motor vehicle distribution and repairs, fuel	0.0	0.2	0.5	0.5	0.8
Wholesale distribution	2.1	2.8	2.7	2.4	3.8
Retail distribution	4.1	4.2	4.2	4.1	4.4
Hotels and restaurants	1.3	1.6	1.8	1.9	3.1
Land transport and transport via pipelines	4.8	4.8	4.8	3.9	4.3
Water transport	4.3	2.3	0.5	0.4	0.3
Air transport	1.1	1.1	0.6	1.7	2.2
Ancillary transport services	0.6	0.8	1.5	2.1	3.4
Post and tele-communications	6.0	5.1	5.0	6.7	6.1
Financial intermediation	2.4	2.2	4.6	2.9	2.2
Insurance and pension funds	0.3	0.7	1.8	1.1	2.0
Auxiliary financial services	0.0	0.0	0.3	0.4	0.5
Real estate activities	1.0	1.7	2.7	2.6	5.6
Renting of machinery etc	0.7	1.9	1.8	2.8	2.9
Computer services	0.0	0.0	0.3	1.3	1.1
Research and development	0.0	0.0	0.1	0.3	0.4
Other business services	0.5	0.8	2.8	4.3	3.1
Public administration and defence	10.4	7.1	13.0	9.4	9.8
Education	3.1	3.2	2.1	2.8	2.0
Health and social work	1.0	1.1	1.1	2.4	1.2
Sewage and sanitary services	0.5	0.6	1.8	2.3	2.8
Membership organisations	0.0	0.1	0.2	0.2	0.2
Recreational services	1.8	2.4	2.8	4.0	4.6
Other services activities	0.0	0.1	0.3	0.4	0.3
All services industries	46.0	44.8	57.4	60.6	67.1

CONTACT

 elmr@ons.gsi.gov.uk

REFERENCES

Chamberlin G, Clayton T and Farooqui S (2007) 'New measures of UK private sector software investment', *Economic & Labour Market Review* 1(5), pp 17–28 and at www.statistics.gov.uk/cci/article.asp?id=1798

Dean G (1964) 'The Stock of Fixed Capital in the United Kingdom in 1961', *Journal of the Royal Statistical Society, Series A (General)* Vol. 127, No. 3, pp 327–58.

Giorgio Marrano M, Haskel J and Wallis G (2007) 'What Happened to the Knowledge Economy? ICT, Intangible Investment and Britain's Productivity Record Revisited', *Queen Mary College Working Paper* 603.

Goodridge P (2006) 'Experimental quality-adjusted labour input measure – 1996 to 2005', *Economic Trends* 637 pp 46–56 and at www.statistics.gov.uk/cci/article.asp?id=1693

Goodridge P (2007) 'Multi-factor productivity analysis', *Economic & Labour Market Review*, 1(7) pp 32–38 and at www.statistics.gov.uk.cci/article.asp?id=1826

Griffin T (1975) 'Revised estimates of the consumption and stock of fixed capital', *Economic Trends* 264, pp 126–9. Available on request from elmr@ons.gsi.gov.uk

Hall R E and Jorgenson D W (1967) 'Tax Policy and Investment Behaviour', *American Economic Review* Vol. 57, No. 3, pp 391–414.

Hulten C R and Wykoff F C (1981a) 'The estimate of economic depreciation using vintage asset prices'. *Journal of Econometrics* Vol. 57, pp 367–96.

Hulten C R and Wykoff F C (1981b) 'The measurement of economic depreciation', In Hulten C R (Ed), *Depreciation, inflation and the taxation of income from capital*. The Urban Institute Press.

Jorgenson D W (1963) 'Capital Theory and Investment Behaviour', *American Economic Review* Vol. 53, No. 2, pp 247–59.

Jorgenson D W and Griliches Z (1967) 'The explanation of productivity change', *Review of Economic Studies* Vol. 34, No. 3, pp 249–83.

Marks K (2007) 'Market sector GVA productivity measures', *Economic & Labour Market Review* 1(3), pp 47–53 and at www.statistics.gov.uk/cci/article.asp?id=1742

Organisation for Economic Co-operation and Development (2001) Measuring Capital – OECD Manual.

Office for National Statistics (2007) *The ONS Productivity Handbook: A Statistical Overview and Guide.* Palgrave Macmillan: Basingstoke.

Oulton N and Srinivasan S (2003) 'Capital stocks, capital services, and depreciation: an integrated framework', *Bank of England Working Paper* No. 192, available at www.bankofengland.co.uk/publications/workingpapers/wp192.pdf

Wallis G (2005) 'Estimates of the volume of capital services', *Economic Trends* 624, pp 42–51 and at www.statistics.gov.uk/cci/article.asp?id=1297

FEATURE

Catrin Ormerod
Office for National Statistics

What is known about numbers and 'earnings' of the self-employed?

SUMMARY

There is currently very little information available about the so-called 'earnings' of the self-employed, particularly because by definition they do not earn a salary or wage.

This article firstly identifies the self-employed in a number of different sources using two perspectives: the individual perspective obtained through self-classification in household surveys and the legal perspective set out by HM Revenue and Customs (HMRC). This work suggests that self-classification as self-employed in household surveys can be adjusted towards the legal perspective using information on the types of self-employment and payment of tax and National Insurance.

The 'earnings' of the self-employed are then examined using information from household surveys and compared with aggregate figures published by HMRC.

There is a wealth of information on earnings in the UK, mainly collected by the Office for National Statistics (ONS) (see Ormerod, 2006a). Earnings and pay refer to the remuneration (wages and salaries) provided directly by employers to employees in return for their supplied labour. Those who own and operate their own business or professional practice, sometimes in conjunction with a partner, are considered as self-employed, although this is only one aspect of the perception of self-employment. By definition, therefore, the self-employed do not receive any earnings because they do not supply any labour to an employer.

Consequently, people who are self-employed do not generally appear in estimates of 'earnings', although clearly they are earning an income. The concept of the 'earnings' of the self-employed therefore exists although it has not been clearly defined; information on the 'earnings' of the self-employed is largely an unmet need.

National Accounts estimates the impact of self-employed 'earnings' on the economy as the 'mixed income' component of the income measure of gross domestic product (GDP(I)). Another ONS project is currently in the process of comparing labour market sources of information on the 'earnings' of the self-employed with mixed income figures from National Accounts. Labour market sources therefore have a missing set of 'earnings' for a group. It is difficult to make an assessment of the contribution

of this group and to assess their impact on the labour market. This article aims to shed some light on this issue by examining a range of sources in a consistent framework.

A number of difficulties are involved in measuring the 'earnings' of the self-employed, not least what is meant by this term. The first, and fundamental issue, is the definition of the self-employed themselves. It is not possible to ascertain the 'earnings' for this group if they cannot first be identified.

There is no single definition of the self-employed. This investigation therefore starts by examining various perceptions of the self-employed and linking these to sources of information. A number of investigations have been carried out into the definition of the self-employed (see Burchell, Deakin and Honey (1999) for an example) but there has been no comprehensive review of the information that is available on the self-employed. ONS has also carried out work in this area, in the 'Review of Employment and Jobs Statistics' (ONS, 2006a) and most recently the 'Review of Workforce Jobs Benchmarking' (ONS, 2007).

This article brings together the sources of information on the numbers and 'earnings' of the self-employed for the first time. This investigation is then expanded to identify self-employed individuals in surveys that also hold information on 'earnings'. The definition of the 'earnings' of the self-employed is then investigated and sources of information on these 'earnings' are assessed.

Definitions and sources
Who are the self-employed?

There is no clear definition of the self-employed. Broadly there appear to be two perspectives on the definition, the legal aspect and the view of the individual. The legal perspective may change, but individuals' perceptions of their status often do not accompany this change.

HM Revenue and Customs (HMRC) collects tax from the self-employed and therefore needs to identify these individuals. Guidelines are laid out by HMRC and the Employment Rights Act of 1996[1] to identify the characteristics of the self-employed. However, in any dispute or tribunal, the decision ultimately rests with the courts and they generally follow their own guidance by applying case law to the individual's situation. A legal definition of the self-employed does not therefore exist but HMRC sets out guidance to allow individuals to classify themselves as self-employed based a number of questions. If an individual answers 'yes' to all of the following questions, it will usually mean that they are self-employed:

- can they hire someone to do the work or engage helpers at their own expense?
- do they risk their own money?
- do they provide the main items of equipment they need to do their job, not just the small tools that many employees provide for themselves?
- do they agree to do a job for a fixed price regardless of how long the job may take?
- can they decide what work to do, how and when to do the work and where to provide the services?
- do they regularly work for a number of different people?
- do they have to correct unsatisfactory work in their own time and at their own expense?

Due to the absence of a definition, these statements attempt to reflect the characteristics of people who are usually considered to be self-employed. None of the statements alone characterises an individual as self-employed. For example, many employees tend to work for a number of different people; however, for the self-employed, this is generally the case as they work for a number of different customers to maximise profit.

The International Labour Organisation (ILO) definition of self-employment jobs is those jobs where the remuneration is directly dependent upon the profits (or the potential for profits) derived from the goods and services produced (where own consumption is considered to be part of profits). The incumbents make the operational decisions affecting the enterprise, or delegate such decisions while retaining responsibility for the welfare of the enterprise. (In this context 'enterprise' includes one-person operations.)

Generally, in household surveys, individuals classify themselves as employed or self-employed. This particularly applies to the Labour Force Survey (LFS) which is collected according to the ILO definition in line with international guidelines; however, as this is not read out by the interviewer, it has no operational status. Put simply, generally the household surveys' definition of the self-employed is anyone who believes themselves to be so. There are a number of areas where the legal perception of the self-employed is inconsistent with individuals' perceptions.

For example, sole directors of limited companies are often entrepreneurs who have set up their own companies and in effect feel they are working for themselves. However, the company pays the director a salary or wage and HMRC would consider the individual to be an employee. Other groups of individuals are paid by agencies but consider themselves to be self-employed.

It can generally be assumed that if tax and National Insurance (NI) are deducted from an individual's salary before they are paid, then the individual is an employee according to the legal perspective. This may therefore be another way of adjusting figures on the self-classified self-employed to provide measures in line with the legal perspective. Some individuals, especially those who are subcontractors, may have income tax or National Insurance payments deducted at source (but not both) by whoever contracts them. In some cases, for example actors, NI is deducted but tax is not. If information on tax and NI is to be used to adjust the self-classification of the self-employed, this needs to take this difference into account.

The need to identify certain groups of individuals as employed or self-employed depends on the analysis required. ONS produces workforce jobs estimates which count the number of jobs in the economy.[2] It is the sum of employee jobs (measured by surveys of employers), self-employment jobs (from the Labour Force Survey (LFS)), those in HM Forces, and government-supported trainees (from administrative sources). ONS identified the double counting of individuals in the workforce jobs figures during the 'Review of Employment and Jobs Statistics' (ONS, 2006a). This was also considered during the 'Review of Workforce Jobs Benchmarking' (ONS, 2007). This double counting is due to individuals appearing in business surveys and self-classifying themselves as self-employed in the LFS. Evidence from the LFS suggests that self-employment may be over-reported. In particular, many people classify their main job as self-employed but they subsequently say that they are the sole director of a limited company and/or are paid by an agency, which suggests that they are employees.

Other analyses on the numbers of the self-employed may require these individuals to be included. The focus here is not on deciding which perspective is the correct one, but on identifying individuals according to the different perspectives, so that appropriate analysis can take place. The 'Review of Workforce Jobs Benchmarking' (ONS, 2007) made one recommendation relating to the reporting of the self-employed: ONS should consider, with others, whether there is a suitable source for 'self-employment from a business perspective' that can complement the workforce jobs estimate of employee jobs. This definition of the self-employed would be equivalent to the legal perception discussed above.

The ONS labour cost framework identifies the 'earnings' of the self-employed as an area where there is currently little information (Ormerod, 2006b). There is interest in the impact of this group but no clear requirement at the moment for a particular type of analysis. Possible analyses could fall into a number of areas. There may be interest in the earnings from the legal or individual's perspective. This information could be derived from a number of sources depending on the requirement. An interest in the 'earnings' of entrepreneurs for example could be examined by looking at three areas: the basic income in ASHE of sole directors (this would exclude the majority of their income which appears as profit), the 'earnings' information of self-employed sole directors from household surveys or the profits of companies in business data. This article therefore reviews the information available on these 'earnings' and describes an initial analysis of this information to examine the quality and availability of data in this area.

Information from household surveys

Labour Force Survey (LFS)

The UK LFS[3] is the main source used by ONS to measure the numbers of the self-employed. The LFS is a survey of households living at private addresses in the UK. It is the main source for information on the labour market in the UK. It is a survey of approximately 53,000 households every three months. As well as private households, the survey includes people living in student residence halls[4] and NHS accommodation. Estimates of the numbers of self-employed jobs are obtained from the LFS to contribute to the workforce jobs estimates.

The LFS asks people 'Were you working as an employee or were you self-employed?' The individual can respond employee, self-employed, government scheme or unpaid family worker.

Those who respond as self-employed (and 'employees' who are not paid a salary or wage) can select up to four of the following sub-classifications in a follow-on question:

- paid a salary or a wage by an agency
- sole director of their own limited business
- running a business or a professional practice
- a partner in a business or a professional practice
- working for themselves
- a subcontractor
- doing freelance work

Work carried out during the review of workforce jobs involved estimating the overcounting in the workforce jobs estimate due to sole directors of limited companies and agency workers using this information. To date, official estimates of the self-employed have not been produced on the legal perspective from the LFS as international requirements state that self-classification should be used. The next section attempts to use follow-on information to adjust the figures of the self-classified self-employed towards the legal perspective in order to allow alternative analyses.

The issue of double counting self-reporting for self-employed individuals was identified during the 'Review of Employment and Jobs Statistics' (ONS, 2006a). This resulted in the development of a new question to try and identify further individuals who appear in household and business surveys based on the payment of tax and NI.

In 2005 an LFS pilot was carried out which asked respondents who was responsible for the payment of their income tax or own NI contribution. The aim of the question is to allow the number of respondents to be identified who state that they are self-employed but their income tax is paid through a PAYE scheme. Cognitive testing showed that the question was generally understood by the respondents. However, further discussions by experts suggested that the wording of the question should be changed. The question was implemented in 2007 and is worded, 'Do you pay your own NI and tax or is this usually deducted by the organisation(s) you work for, for example, your client, employer, agency etc?' The use of 'and' instead of 'or' eliminates certain employed individuals who pay their own tax or NI but not both, for example actors. The possible responses to the question implemented are:

- pay own NI and tax
- pay own NI or tax but not both
- NI and tax is deducted by organisation

Information from this question is not yet available for analysis. Once the information is available, ONS will be carrying out an initial analysis before releasing the information to researchers.

Information on self-employed from the LFS is published in the LFS quarterly supplement and is also available in the Labour Market Statistics first release and on NOMIS.[5] In the LFS quarterly supplement, the data are provided quarterly and are broken down by sex, part-time and full-time, occupation, socio-economic classification, industry and hours worked.[6]

When an individual self-classifies as self-employed, the respondent is not asked for any information on hours or earnings as these are outside the scope of the survey. Despite the LFS being the main source of information on the self-employed, it cannot be used to examine their 'earnings'.

Family Resources Survey

The Family Resources Survey (FRS)[7] is a continuous survey of private households and was commissioned by the Department for Work and Pensions (DWP). The survey started in 1992 to meet the specific information requirements of DWP and was designed to provide information about living standards and examine how people interact with the social security system.

A Family Resources Survey Publication[8] is produced from the FRS which provides figures on the total number of self-employed as a percentage of its sample size. The data are broken down by age, ethnicity and region. The FRS does not produce any statistical outputs of the earnings of the self-employed but has been used as a source for earnings information in analyses in the past. 'Self-employment in the UK labour market', Weir (2003) is one such example.

The FRS differs from the LFS as the interviewer attempts to move the self-employed classification towards the legal or 'business' perspective using guidance and checking questions. Initially, individuals in the FRS are asked to classify themselves as self-employed using the question, 'Are you working as an employee or self-employed (including Business Start-Up)'. Within the survey, self-employed people are considered to be working if they work in their own business, professional practice or firm for the purpose of earning a profit even if the enterprise is failing to make a profit or is just being set up.

There are a number of checking questions included in the FRS which result in some individuals initially self-classifying as self-employed then being reclassified as employees. These checking questions do not result in all responses being classified in the same way, so it is possible to maintain the original classification even if the checking question suggests this may be incorrect. However, the original response is not recorded for those which are changed. The FRS can therefore be adjusted further using the checking questions. There is also a follow-on question where individuals are asked to describe the situation that best describes them and can select one from the following list:

- employee
- running a business or professional practice
- partner in a business or professional practice
- working for myself
- a subcontractor
- doing freelance work
- self-employed in some other way

Those responding with the last six descriptions are then asked 'In this job/business are/were you the director of a limited company?' If the individual responds positively, then a checking question is included to ask whether the respondent is on the PAYE system and do they get a payslip. If the respondent answers yes then their response to the classification question may be changed to 'employee' on probing. In order to distinguish directors who are self-employed from those who are employees, an additional question is asked of this group, 'In this job/business are your National Insurance contributions deducted at source?' Except under special circumstances, responding positively to this question results in the individual being coded as an employee.

In order to further distinguish the self-employed from employees, an additional question on tax is included, 'Is either income tax or your regular National Insurance contribution deducted at source?' Respondents can reply 'Income tax deducted', 'Regular NI deducted' or 'No, neither deducted'. This question can be used in a similar way to the new LFS question to identify those who are not self-employed from the legal perspective but self-classify as self-employed. The question does not allow for individuals whose tax and NI are deducted at source to be identified, therefore some of these may still be classified as self-employed from the legal perspective, where their tax or NI, but not both, is deducted at source.

The FRS includes the following information on 'earnings' for all the respondents who classify themselves as self-employed:

- individuals' share of profit or loss figure shown on the accounts
- income from the business for non-business purposes. This includes drawings from the bank/building society and income for the business that is not channelled through the bank/building society account (for example, cash in hand)
- income from the job/business. This means money from the job/business that is used for personal, domestic, non-business use. In other words, what the respondent has to live on

British Household Panel Survey
The main objective of the British Household Panel Survey (BHPS) is to improve understanding of social and economic change in Britain. The BHPS has interviewed members of the same sample of households annually since 1991; it had an original sample size in 1991 of 5,500 households. The total sample size is now around 9,000 households across the UK, providing annual interviews with some 15,000 individuals. All adults over 16 years old are interviewed in the household. The BHPS is carried out by the Institute of Social and Economic Research based at the University of Essex. Access is available through the UK Data Archive.[9]

Individuals are asked to classify themselves as employed or self-employed.

A follow-on question is also included; however, it is not in the same form as the LFS and FRS. Respondents must select one of the following descriptions which best describes their employment situation:

- running a business or a professional practice
- partner in a business or a professional practice
- working for myself
- a subcontractor
- doing freelance work
- self-employed in some other way

The BHPS also contains an additional follow-on question. Respondents classifying themselves as self-employed are asked whether they run their own business or professional practice or usually work for other people or organisations but on a self-employed basis. There is no equivalent question present on the LFS or FRS.

Information on 'earnings' is collected through two questions:

- how much net profit did you make from your share of the business or practice?
- how much did you earn (before tax) in the last twelve months or the most recent period for which you have figures?

Comparison of data sources on the self-employed
Information on the numbers and earnings of the self-employed therefore covers a number of areas across the LFS, FRS and BHPS. These are compared in **Table 1**.

The first area is in self-classification. Generally, respondents are not provided with a definition to work with but are expected to understand the differences between employment and self-employment. This is in line with international requirements.

The FRS differs from the LFS and BHPS by attempting to move the self-classification towards a legal or business perspective using checking questions. It is important to note that the original response is not recorded if it is adjusted following a checking question, so it is not possible to analyse this. The FRS uses one of the areas where classification is known to be vague, for directors of companies, to attempt to remove misclassification. The LFS and BHPS do not carry out any type of checking on the self-classification question. The LFS applies this method in order to respond to international requirements. Comparison of the numbers classified as self-employed

across the three surveys must therefore consider the differences in definitions at the margins of this group. Generally, these are the figures quoted from the sources for the numbers of the self-employed.

ONS has estimated the extent of overcounting in workforce jobs due to individuals being classified as self-employed in the LFS and also appearing in business surveys as employees. It might therefore be possible to produce alternative estimates of the self-employed, according to the legal perspective, by excluding certain groups of individuals from the set which self-classify as self-employed, if this better met some analytical purposes. ONS will always continue to publish the self-classified estimate while this is in line with international requirements.

It is possible to remove types of self-employment that are usually perceived by the individual to be self-employment but legally as employed: the sole directors of limited companies and those who are paid a wage or salary by an agency. For the FRS and LFS, this adjustment is comparable, as the question on the type of self-employment covers the same categories, although some of this adjustment has been carried out during the interview for the FRS. For the BHPS, this is assumed to be those in the 'other' category. Analysis of the numbers of individuals in these groups is consistent across the surveys so this assumption seems to be sensible. Reconciliation of the follow-on questions for the self-employed across the three surveys is shown in **Table 2**.

Information on the payment of tax and NI can be used to further identify the difference between the individual and legal perception of self-employed. This information can be used to further adjust the numbers of the self-classified self-employed towards the legal perspective.

The FRS includes a question on tax and NI payment. Since the beginning of 2007, the LFS has also included a question on tax and NI. Discussion with experts in this area suggests that, from the legal perspective, the self-employed are those who pay their own tax and NI and not just one or the other. The two questions differ across the surveys. The LFS question has been designed specifically to address the double counting in workforce jobs figures and therefore allows those who pay both tax and NI to be identified. The FRS only allows individuals who pay both or either to be identified. Information from the FRS question is currently available and can be examined; information from the LFS is due to be examined by ONS before being released to researchers.

Table 1
Comparison of questions on employment status as self-employed and earnings of the 'self-employed' from household surveys

	Labour Force Survey LFS	Family Resources Survey FRS	British Household Panel Survey BHPS
Self-classification question	● Were you working as an employee or were you self-employed? 1: Employee 2: Self-employed 3: Government scheme 4: Unpaid family worker	● Are you working as 1: An employee 2: Self-employed (including Business Start-Up)	● Are you an employee or self-employed? 1: Employee 2: Self-employed
Checking questions	● None	● Those responding with descriptions 2–7 for type of self-employment are asked: In this job/business were/are you the director of a limited company? If Yes following checking questions asked ● Are they on PAYE? Do they/would they get a payslip? If yes then classification is changed to 'Employee' ● In this job/business, are your National Insurance contributions deducted at source? Generally if yes then classification is changed to 'Employee'	● None
Follow-on questions	● Respondent can select up to four from: 1: Paid a salary or a wage by an agency 2: Sole director of their own limited business 3: Running a business or a professional practice 4: A partner in a business or a professional practice 5: Working for themselves 6: A subcontractor 7: Doing freelance work	● Respondent must select one from: 1: Employee 2: Running a business or professional practice 3: Partner in a business or professional practice 4: Working for myself 5: A subcontractor 6: Doing freelance work 7: Self-employed in some other way ● Those responding with descriptions 2–7 are then asked: In this job/business are/were you the director of a limited company? (same as first checking question)	● Respondent must select one which best describes their employment situation 1: Running a business or a professional practice 2: Partner in a business or a professional practice 3: Working for myself 4: A subcontractor 5: Doing freelance work 6: Self-employed in some other way ● You said you are self-employed. Does this mean that you run your own business or professional practice or do you usually work for other people or organisations but on a self-employed basis?
Tax/NI question	● Do you pay your own National Insurance or tax or are these usually deducted by the organisation(s) you work for, for example, your client, employer, agency etc.? 1: Pay own NI and tax 2: Pay own NI or tax but not both 3: NI and tax is deducted by organisation	● Is either income tax, or your regular National Insurance contribution deducted at source? 1: Income tax deducted 2: Regular NI deducted 3: No, neither deducted	● None
Earnings information	● None	● What was (your share of) the profit or loss figure shown on these accounts for this period ● How much have you taken for non-business purposes? ● Apart from any drawings from the bank/building society, how much income from this job/business, for personal use? ● On average, what was your income from your job/business: that is, after paying for any materials, equipment or goods that you use(d) in your work?	● How much net profit did you make from your share of the business or practice? ● How much did you earn (before tax) in the last twelve months or the most recent period for which you have figures?

If the FRS tax and NI question is used to identify individuals who are legally perceived to be self-employed, this will be an overestimate of the adjustment required as it is not possible to identify those who pay both their own tax and NI.

It has been recognised that, while information on tax and NI payment is useful in determining who is self-employed in terms of the legal perspective, sole directors of limited companies may respond to this question in a different way to others. Sole directors of limited companies will classify themselves as self-employed, although from the legal perspective they would be classified as employees. Any adjustment towards the legal perspective would therefore exclude these individuals. On responding to a question on tax and NI, these directors then often say that they pay both themselves. It

is probably the case that these individuals pay tax and NI on behalf of their company as they have this responsibility. Any categorisation of these individuals according to the legal perspective should therefore probably still exclude this group despite their response to the tax question.

Figure 1 shows the possible adjusting process for the household surveys using questions on types of self-employment and tax.

Table 2
Reconciliation of types of self-employment questions across household surveys

Labour Force Survey LFS	Family Resources Survey FRS	British Household Panel Survey BHPS
1: Paid a salary or a wage by an agency 2: Sole director of their own limited business	7: Self-employed in some other way Those responding with descriptions 2–7 are asked: In this job/business are/were you the director of a limited company? (same as first checking question)	6: Self-employed in some other way
3: Running a business or a professional practice	2: Running a business or professional practice	1: Running a business or a professional practice
4: A partner in a business or a professional practice	3: Partner in a business or a professional practice	2: Partner in a business or a professional practice
5: Working for themselves	4: Working for myself	3: Working for myself
6: A subcontractor	5: A subcontractor	4: A subcontractor
7: Doing freelance work	6: Doing freelance work	5: Doing freelance work

HMRC counts of the self-employed

HMRC holds information on the numbers and `earnings' of the self-employed on their administrative systems. In the case of a dispute, courts decide on whether an individual is an employee or self-employed. In the majority of cases, HMRC guidelines are used and these are the source of the legal perspective. Self-employed individuals are included according to whether (and how many) sets of pages covering income from trades or from partnerships were completed in the tax return. Such pages are required for all trades, and for all shares in partnerships, trading at any time in the tax year. An individual with two or more sources of self-employment income (from trades or partnerships) is counted more than once according to the industry group and profit for each source.

There is a possible issue with the information on `earnings' from HMRC as this is likely to under-report the earnings of the self-employed because it is based on official tax returns. There is anecdotal evidence to suggest that some of the self-employed illegally fail to disclose all of their earnings information to HMRC. There are also long lags involved in tax collection with the self-employed. As a result, figures may respond slowly to changes in the economy.

National Accounts provides detailed estimates of national product, income and expenditure for the UK. Data are available for the aggregate level of `earnings' for the self-employed; this information is derived mainly from HMRC. This is provided under mixed income in the National Accounts (for the most recent information, see ONS, 2006b). The National Accounts defines mixed income as the balancing item on the generation of income account for unincorporated businesses owned by households. The owner or members of the same household often provide unpaid labour inputs to the business. The surplus is therefore a mixture of remuneration for such labour and return to the owner as entrepreneur.

The method of measuring the self-employed is based on the characteristics

Figure 1
Possible adjustments to household data sources to the classification of the self-employed

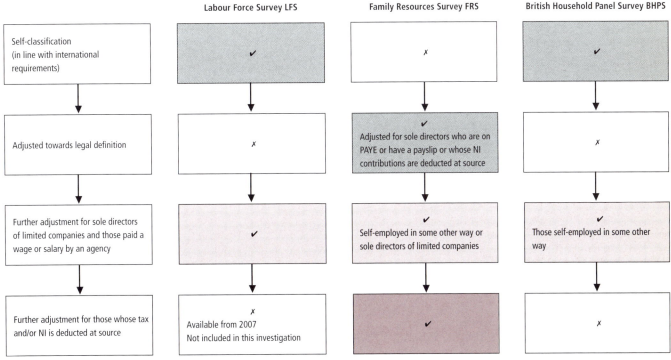

Note:
Comparable definitions across three surveys are shown in the same colour

of the business rather than the opinion of the individual and this is therefore more likely to tie in with the legal perspective of the self-employed. Mixed income in the National Accounts is based on the income of the household and therefore accounts for any labour provided by other household members. However, this should not be of operational importance because the data are only provided in aggregate form for the whole economy. When comparing this with aggregated figures from sources derived at the individual level, there should not be any difference in the results.

Numbers of self-employed

Table 3 shows the numbers of the self-employed weighted to the total population according to self-classification and adjusted towards the legal perspective. The LFS and FRS data sets both contain weights; the BHPS is simply weighted using the proportions of the self-employed and employed to the LFS total population.

The LFS is the main source for the numbers of the self-employed and shows that there are around 3.5 million self-classified self-employed jobs. The numbers self-classified as self-employed are very similar across the three sources. This is despite the fact that the FRS carries out on-the-spot validation to try to reclassify some individuals towards the legal perspective.

Adjusting the self-classification, by removing individuals who are sole directors or are paid by an agency, produces an estimate of the self-employed, according to the legal perspective, which is 10 per cent less than the self-classified value, according to the LFS and FRS. This adjustment is less using the BHPS, at around 4 per cent. The follow-up question on the type of self-employment could account for this difference, as the only way to classify sole directors or agency workers using the BHPS is to remove all individuals classified as 'self-employed in some other way' (see Table 2).

The FRS information on the payment of tax or NI at source suggests a further reduction of 25 per cent. This seems high, especially in light of information from the pilot LFS question which suggests a much lower level of adjustment; however, it is based on a very small sample size. This cannot therefore be used to improve the estimate of overcounting of self-employment, but it does seem likely that the estimate should be enhanced when results from the LFS using this new question become available. Further work is currently being carried out to examine the new LFS question. This will be published in 2007.

The FRS adjustment is likely to be too high as it removes certain groups who pay tax or NI who legally would be described as employees. This cannot be used to indicate overcounting by the LFS, as the surveys are conducted differently, with different questions, but it tends to confirm that overestimation of self-employment in surveys is a significant issue.

Earnings of the self-employed

The LFS is thought to be the most reliable source of information on the number of the self-employed. However, as discussed, the LFS does not collect any information on the 'earnings' of the self-employed. The other household sources therefore need to be used as these do include information on income and profit from self-employment.

Figure 2 shows the average gross annual earnings of those self-categorised as self-employed, using HMRC figures, National Accounts information and household surveys. National Accounts information is derived from HMRC and these sources therefore provide similar levels of average earnings.

FRS information on average earnings appears to be unrealistically low; this is an acknowledged issue with the FRS. Information for the BHPS is closer to the official HMRC figure, particularly for those who are classified as full-time self-employed. BHPS questions on earnings are simpler than FRS questions and this could account for the better-quality information obtained from the BHPS. The 'earnings' information presented here from household surveys is based on the self-classification. It is also possible to examine earnings

Table 3
Numbers of self-employed jobs according to self-classification and legal perspective

	Source	Data set	Thousands			Percentage change	
			Self-classified as self-employed[1] (A)	Adjusted for sole directors and those paid by an agency[2] (B)	Adjusted for sole directors and those paid by an agency and those not paying their own tax or NI[3] (C)	(B)/(A)	(C)/(B)
2005	LFS	Spring 05	3,565	3,197	–	−10.3	–
	FRS	2004/05	3,382	3,061	2,308	−9.5	−24.6
	BHPS	2004	3,400	3,290	–	−3.2	–
2004	LFS	Spring 04	3,564	3,244	–	−9.0	–
	FRS	2003/04	3,292	2,974	2,239	−9.7	−24.7
	BHPS	2003	3,405	3,241	–	−4.8	–
2003	LFS	Spring 03	3,411	3,272	–	−4.1	–
	FRS	2002/03	3,201	2,924	2,212	−8.6	−24.4
	BHPS	2002	3,188	3,070	–	−3.7	–

Notes:

1 FRS includes on-the-spot validation
2 For BHPS this is self-employed in some other way
3 Likely to be an underestimate as those who pay their own tax or NI but not both excluded
– Not applicable
LFS: spring quarter March to May
FRS: financial year March to April
BHPS: calendar year January to December

Figure 2
Average gross annual earnings of the self-employed

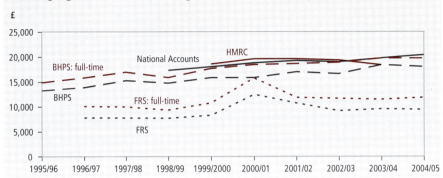

excluding those who would legally be perceived as self-employed. Initial analysis shows that average earnings based on the legal perspective are lower.

It may have been expected that tax information on the self-employed held by HMRC would underestimate earnings, as anecdotal evidence suggests that some individuals fail to declare some earnings. This is not corroborated by information from household surveys (although this is still likely to be the case). This suggests that further work is required to clarify the 'earnings' questions for the self-employed from household surveys, to ensure all sources are included. This also suggests that, currently, the HMRC is the best source of information on the 'earnings' of the self-employed.

However, HMRC information is only provided at aggregate level. The similarity between information from the HMRC and BHPS, particularly for the full-time self-employed, suggests that the BHPS could be used as a source of individual level information to carry out more detailed analysis than is possible at the macro level. Sample sizes are, however, small and this issue needs to be considered when attempting to carry out any analysis of different groups.

Conclusion

Before this investigation, little was known about the 'earnings' of the self-employed; this article brings together the sources of information on the numbers and earnings of the self-employed for the first time. There are two perspectives on this information:

- the individuals' perspective generally obtained from household surveys where self-classification takes place, and
- the legal perspective by which HMRC publishes information

Neither perspective is the 'correct' one. International regulations require published estimates of the self-employed to be based on self-classification, but there may be instances where estimates could be required from the legal perspective. It is possible to adjust the self-classified estimates using additional information provided in household surveys, to provide estimates from the legal perspective, and these are presented here.

Part of this adjustment involves examining whether individuals pay their own tax and NI. Currently this information is only available from the FRS and suggests that the difference between the individual and legal perspective is quite large. ONS is due to publish information on this basis from the LFS, which is based on new information collected from 2007. Dress rehearsal of the LFS question suggested a much smaller difference than presented here for the FRS. This could partly be due to the difference in the FRS and LFS question. The difference suggested by the FRS is greater than the true value as it includes individuals who legally would be considered as employees despite paying either their own tax or NI. Further work is required to examine this following publication of the new LFS information.

There is some interest in the 'earnings' of these individuals. Identifying them according to either perspective allows analysis to be carried out on the required set of individuals. This is currently only possible at individual level using the FRS and BHPS. Aggregate information is provided by HMRC and, through the National Accounts, this information is provided from the legal perspective. Initial investigations show that FRS information on the self-employed is understated. Information from the BHPS can be reconciled with aggregate HMRC figures,

particularly when looking at the full-time self-employed. It should therefore be possible to carry out further analysis of the earnings of the self-employed using this source although the small sample size needs to be considered.

Clearly there is no single consistent source of information on the 'earnings' of the self-employed. Further analysis is possible using available sources but this requires more consultation with users to determine the precise need for this information.

Notes

1 See HMRC guidance on employment status at www.hmrc.gov.uk/employment-status/index.htm#1

2 Estimates of workforce jobs can be accessed from www.statistics.gov.uk/statbase/product.asp?vlnk=9765

3 For more information on the LFS see www.statistics.gov.uk/statbase/source.asp?vlnk=358

4 Students in halls are only included by being picked up through having parents who are sampled as being part of the resident population of UK households. Students in halls with parents living abroad would not be covered.

5 NOMIS gives the public free access to the most detailed and most up-to-date UK labour market statistics from official sources at www.nomisweb.co.uk

6 Published LFS tables can be found at www.statistics.gov.uk/statbase/product.asp?vlnk=545

7 For more information on the FRS see www.statistics.gov.uk/ssd/surveys/survey_family_resources.asp

8 Published information on the FRS can be found at www.dwp.gov.uk/asd/frs/index/publications.asp

9 The UK Data Archive is a centre of expertise in data acquisition, preservation, dissemination and promotion. For more information see www.data-archive.ac.uk

CONTACT

✉ elmr@ons.gsi.gov.uk

REFERENCES

Burchell B, Deakin S, Honey S (1999) 'The employment status of individuals in non-standard employment' at www.dti.gov.uk/files/file11628.pdf

Office for National Statistics (2006a) 'National Statistics Quality Review Series Report No. 44: Review of Employment and Jobs Statistics' at www.statistics.gov.uk/about/data/methodology/quality/reviews/downloads/ejr_final.pdf

Office for National Statistics (2006b) 'United Kingdom National Accounts: The Blue Book 2006' at www.statistics.gov.uk/downloads/theme_economy/bluebook2006.pdf

Office for National Statistics (2007) 'Review of Workforce Jobs Benchmarking' at www.statistics.gov.uk/downloads/theme_labour/wfjreport.pdf

Ormerod C (2006a) 'Earnings data: A brief guide to sources and outputs', *Labour Market Trends* (114)11, pp 389–96 and at www.statistics.gov.uk/downloads/theme_labour/lmt_nov06.pdf

Ormerod C (2006b) 'A framework for Labour Costs Statistics', *Labour Market Trends* (114)6, pp 203–11 and at www.statistics.gov.uk/downloads/theme_labour/lmt_jun06.pdf

Weir G (2003) 'Self-employment in the UK labour market', *Labour Market Trends* (111)9, pp 441–52 and at www.statistics.gov.uk/downloads/theme_labour/lmt_september03.pdf

FEATURE

Ian Richardson
Office for National Statistics

Services producer price index (experimental) – first quarter 2007

SUMMARY

The experimental services producer price index (SPPI) measures movements in prices charged for services supplied by businesses to other businesses, local and national government. This article shows the effects some industries are having on the top-level SPPI. It continues the quarterly feature previously published in *Economic Trends*. The data produced are used internally by the Office for National Statistics as a deflator for the index of services and the quarterly measurement of gross domestic product. The index is also used by HM Treasury and the Bank of England to help monitor inflation in the economy.

Prices of business-to-business services rose by 2.7 per cent in the year to the first quarter of 2007. This is based on a comparison of the change in the top-level services producer price index (SPPI) on the net sector basis.

Figure 1 shows how the percentage change for the top-level SPPI (net sector) compares with the retail prices index (RPI) all services sector, and the producer price index (PPI) for all manufactured goods (net sector).

The top-level results, on both gross and net sector bases, are shown in **Table 1**. In 2007 Q1, the top-level SPPI (net sector) rose by 0.4 per cent compared with the previous quarter.

Figure 2 depicts the SPPI annual growths for both the net and gross sector time series. The annual growth for the SPPI net sector fell to 2.7 per cent in 2007 Q1, down from 2.9 per cent in 2006 Q4. The gross SPPI growth fell to 2.5 per cent in 2007

Q1 down from 2.6 per cent in the previous quarter. The difference in the annual growth between the gross and net sector SPPI is 0.2 per cent this quarter.

Industry-specific indices

Tables available on the National Statistics website contain the data for the 34 industries for which indices of services producer prices are currently available. The weights for each industry index are shown at both gross and net sector levels. Comparing Q1 2007 with Q1 2006, some key points to note are:

- property rentals rose 4.6 per cent, due to sustained growth within the sector as reported by the Investment Property Databank
- sewerage services prices rose by 8.3 per cent, following rises reported by OFWAT

Figure 1
Experimental top-level SPPI compared with the RPI and PPI

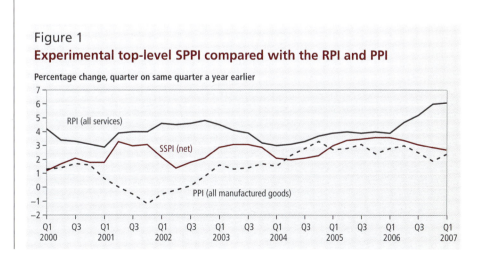

Percentage change, quarter on same quarter a year earlier

Figure 2
Experimental top-level SPPI

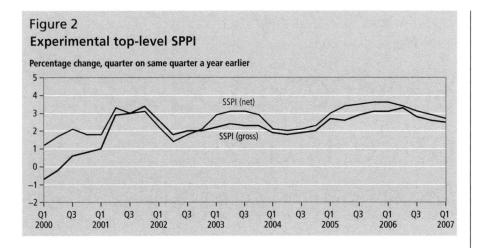

Percentage change, quarter on same quarter a year earlier

Table 1
Top-level SPPI results

	SPPI quarterly index values, 2000=100		Percentage change, quarter on same quarter a year earlier	
	Gross sector	Net sector	Gross sector	Net sector
2000 Q1	100.0	99.5	−0.7	1.2
2000 Q2	99.9	99.8	0.1	1.7
2000 Q3	100.0	100.2	0.7	2.1
2000 Q4	100.1	100.5	0.7	1.8
2001 Q1	100.7	101.3	0.7	1.8
2001 Q2	102.5	103.1	2.6	3.3
2001 Q3	102.8	103.2	2.7	3.0
2001 Q4	103.3	103.6	3.1	3.1
2002 Q1	103.3	103.6	2.7	2.2
2002 Q2	104.4	104.6	1.9	1.4
2002 Q3	104.9	105.0	2.1	1.8
2002 Q4	105.4	105.8	2.1	2.1
2003 Q1	105.7	106.5	2.3	2.9
2003 Q2	107.0	107.9	2.4	3.1
2003 Q3	107.4	108.3	2.4	3.1
2003 Q4	107.8	108.8	2.3	2.9
2004 Q1	107.6	108.7	1.7	2.1
2004 Q2	108.9	110.0	1.8	2.0
2004 Q3	109.4	110.6	1.8	2.1
2004 Q4	109.9	111.3	1.9	2.3
2005 Q1	110.5	112.0	2.7	3.0
2005 Q2	111.7	113.7	2.6	3.4
2005 Q3	112.5	114.5	2.9	3.5
2005 Q4	113.3	115.3	3.1	3.6
2006 Q1	113.9	116.0	3.1	3.6
2006 Q2	115.4	117.6	3.3	3.4
2006 Q3	115.7	118.0	2.8	3.1
2006 Q4	116.3	118.6	2.6	2.9
2007 Q1	116.8	119.1	2.5	2.7

- real estate agency activities rose 11.4 per cent, due to upward price movements reported across the whole of their sector
- employment agencies rose 2.6 per cent, due to a rise in wages·

Next results
The next set of SPPI results will be issued on 22 August 2007 on the National Statistics website at www.statistics.gov.uk/sppi

Further information
All SPPI tables and articles on the methodology and impact of rebasing the SPPI, the redevelopment of an index for business telecommunications and the introduction of an index for banking services (together with more general information on the SPPI) are available at www.statistics.gov.uk/sppi

CONTACT

 elmr@ons.gsi.gov.uk

TECHNICAL NOTE

1 The experimental services producer price index (SPPI) replaces the former corporate services price index (CSPI). It measures movements in prices charged for services supplied by businesses to other businesses, local and national government. It is not classified as a National Statistic.

2 Unless otherwise stated, index numbers shown in the main text are on a net sector basis. These relate only to transactions between the corporate services sector and other sectors. Detailed tables available on the ONS website also contain gross sector indices which include transactions within the corporate services sector.

3 Indices relate to average prices per quarter. The full effect of a price change occurring within a quarter will only be reflected in the index for the following quarter. All index numbers exclude VAT and are not seasonally adjusted.

4 SPPI inflation is the percentage change in the net sector index for the latest quarter compared with the corresponding quarter in the previous year.

5 Grants from the European Commission helped ONS to begin developing the SPPI. Funding of approximately 600,000 euros was awarded between 2002 and 2005. This has now ceased.

6 A number of external data sources are currently used in the compilation of the SPPI, as follows:

Bank of England – banking services

Investment Property Database (IPD) – property rental payments

Office of Communications (Ofcom) – business telecommunications

Office of Water Services (OFWAT) – sewerage services

Parcelforce – national post parcels

Office of Rail Regulation (ORR) – business rail fares

Yew Tree – maintenance and repair of motor vehicles

7 The SPPI for banking has been published since 2003 and is calculated using information from the Bank of England. In 2004 the Bank of England made changes to the forms used to collect data. This led to collection of new data that would facilitate some improvements to the index. However, ONS have been unable to devote the resources to include the new data and from this point these items have been imputed. Recent work has highlighted that inclusion of the new data would lead to significant improvement in the index and therefore the ongoing imputation has led to quality concerns regarding the banking SPPI. Pending further work by ONS to include the effects of the new data within the banking SPPI, ONS plans to withdraw the index from the next release in August 2007.

Key time series

National accounts aggregates

Last updated: 29/06/07

Seasonally adjusted

	£ million		Indices (2003 = 100)							
	At current prices		Value indices at current prices		Chained volume indices			Implied deflators[3]		
	Gross domestic product (GDP) at market prices	Gross value added (GVA) at basic prices	GDP at market prices[1]	GVA at basic prices	Gross national disposable income at market prices[2]	GDP at market prices	GVA at basic prices	GDP at market prices	GVA at basic prices	
	YBHA	ABML	YBEU	YBEX	YBFP	YBEZ	CGCE	YBGB	CGBV	
2001	1,003,297	889,063	89.7	89.5	93.7	95.3	95.6	94.1	93.6	
2002	1,055,793	937,323	94.4	94.3	97.1	97.3	97.3	97.0	97.0	
2003	1,118,245	993,507	100.0	100.0	100.0	100.0	100.0	100.0	100.0	
2004	1,184,296	1,051,934	105.9	105.9	103.4	103.3	103.3	102.6	102.5	
2005	1,233,976	1,096,629	110.3	110.4	104.3	105.2	105.2	104.9	104.9	
2006	1,299,622	1,154,959	116.2	116.3	106.2	108.1	108.2	107.5	107.4	
2001 Q1	247,905	219,532	88.7	88.4	93.1	94.9	95.3	93.5	92.7	
2001 Q2	249,597	220,901	89.3	88.9	93.4	95.0	95.3	94.0	93.3	
2001 Q3	251,028	222,536	89.8	89.6	94.4	95.6	95.8	94.0	93.6	
2001 Q4	254,767	226,094	91.1	91.0	94.1	95.9	96.0	95.0	94.9	
2002 Q1	259,054	229,737	92.7	92.5	95.9	96.4	96.5	96.1	95.9	
2002 Q2	262,774	233,372	94.0	94.0	96.2	97.0	96.9	96.9	97.0	
2002 Q3	265,836	236,103	95.1	95.1	98.3	97.7	97.6	97.4	97.4	
2002 Q4	268,129	238,111	95.9	95.9	98.2	98.2	98.1	97.7	97.7	
2003 Q1	272,953	242,612	97.6	97.7	99.4	98.8	98.8	98.9	98.9	
2003 Q2	277,119	246,427	99.1	99.2	98.9	99.3	99.3	99.8	99.9	
2003 Q3	281,996	250,492	100.9	100.9	100.0	100.4	100.4	100.4	100.5	
2003 Q4	286,177	253,976	102.4	102.3	101.7	101.5	101.6	100.9	100.7	
2004 Q1	288,912	256,106	103.3	103.1	101.9	102.2	102.2	101.1	100.9	
2004 Q2	295,066	262,094	105.5	105.5	103.2	103.1	103.2	102.3	102.3	
2004 Q3	297,941	264,732	106.6	106.6	103.0	103.5	103.5	102.9	103.0	
2004 Q4	302,377	269,002	108.2	108.3	105.4	104.1	104.2	103.9	104.0	
2005 Q1	303,996	270,082	108.7	108.7	104.1	104.4	104.4	104.2	104.1	
2005 Q2	307,306	273,158	109.9	110.0	105.4	104.8	104.9	104.9	104.8	
2005 Q3	308,515	273,676	110.4	110.2	103.5	105.4	105.4	104.7	104.5	
2005 Q4	314,159	279,713	112.4	112.6	104.1	106.1	106.2	106.0	106.1	
2006 Q1	316,789	281,680	113.3	113.4	104.8	106.9	107.0	106.0	106.0	
2006 Q2	321,453	285,500	115.0	114.9	106.9	107.8	107.8	106.7	106.6	
2006 Q3	328,388	291,766	117.5	117.5	106.7	108.5	108.6	108.2	108.2	
2006 Q4	332,992	296,013	119.1	119.2	106.4	109.4	109.5	108.9	108.8	
2007 Q1	336,652	298,773	120.4	120.3	107.9	110.1	110.3	109.3	109.0	

Percentage change, quarter on corresponding quarter of previous year[4]

2001 Q1	5.0	5.3	5.1	5.4	3.3	2.9	2.9	2.1	2.2	
2001 Q2	4.6	5.0	4.6	5.0	3.2	2.3	2.1	2.3	2.8	
2001 Q3	4.1	4.5	4.2	4.6	3.1	2.4	1.9	1.8	2.6	
2001 Q4	4.8	5.2	4.7	5.2	3.7	2.0	1.6	2.7	3.6	
2002 Q1	4.5	4.6	4.5	4.6	3.0	1.6	1.3	2.8	3.5	
2002 Q2	5.3	5.6	5.3	5.7	3.0	2.1	1.7	3.1	4.0	
2002 Q3	5.9	6.1	5.9	6.1	4.1	2.2	1.9	3.6	4.1	
2002 Q4	5.2	5.3	5.3	5.4	4.4	2.4	2.2	2.8	3.0	
2003 Q1	5.4	5.6	5.3	5.6	3.6	2.5	2.4	2.9	3.1	
2003 Q2	5.5	5.6	5.4	5.5	2.8	2.4	2.5	3.0	3.0	
2003 Q3	6.1	6.1	6.1	6.1	1.7	2.8	2.9	3.1	3.2	
2003 Q4	6.7	6.7	6.8	6.7	3.6	3.4	3.6	3.3	3.1	
2004 Q1	5.8	5.6	5.8	5.5	2.5	3.4	3.4	2.2	2.0	
2004 Q2	6.5	6.4	6.5	6.4	4.3	3.8	3.9	2.5	2.4	
2004 Q3	5.7	5.7	5.6	5.6	3.0	3.1	3.1	2.5	2.5	
2004 Q4	5.7	5.9	5.7	5.9	3.6	2.6	2.6	3.0	3.3	
2005 Q1	5.2	5.5	5.2	5.4	2.2	2.2	2.2	3.1	3.2	
2005 Q2	4.1	4.2	4.2	4.3	2.1	1.6	1.6	2.5	2.4	
2005 Q3	3.5	3.4	3.6	3.4	0.5	1.8	1.8	1.7	1.5	
2005 Q4	3.9	4.0	3.9	4.0	−1.2	1.9	1.9	2.0	2.0	
2006 Q1	4.2	4.3	4.2	4.3	0.7	2.4	2.5	1.7	1.8	
2006 Q2	4.6	4.5	4.6	4.5	1.4	2.9	2.8	1.7	1.7	
2006 Q3	6.4	6.6	6.4	6.6	3.1	2.9	3.0	3.3	3.5	
2006 Q4	6.0	5.8	6.0	5.9	2.2	3.1	3.1	2.7	2.5	
2007 Q1	6.3	6.1	6.3	6.1	3.0	3.0	3.1	3.1	2.8	

Notes:

Source: Office for National Statistics

1 "Money GDP".
2 This series is only updated once a quarter, in line with the full quarterly national accounts data set.
3 Based on chained volume measures and current price estimates of expenditure components of GDP.
4 For index number series, these are derived from the rounded figures shown in the table.

Gross domestic product: by category of expenditure

Last updated: 29/06/07

£ million, chained volume measures, reference year 2003, seasonally adjusted

	Domestic expenditure on goods and services at market prices											
	Final consumption expenditure			Gross capital formation								
	Households	Non-profit institutions[1]	General government	Gross fixed capital formation	Changes in inventories[2]	Acquisitions less disposals of valuables	Total	Exports of goods and services	Gross final expenditure	less imports of goods and services	Statistical discrepancy (expenditure)	Gross domestic at product market prices
	ABJR	HAYO	NMRY	NPQT	CAFU	NPJR	YBIM	IKBK	ABMG	IKBL	GIXS	ABMI
2001	653,326	27,155	217,359	178,203	5,577	342	1,082,333	277,694	1,360,205	294,449	0	1,066,217
2002	676,833	27,130	224,868	184,701	2,289	183	1,116,239	280,593	1,396,862	308,706	0	1,088,108
2003	697,160	27,185	232,699	186,700	3,983	−37	1,147,690	285,397	1,433,087	314,842	0	1,118,245
2004	721,434	27,327	240,129	197,655	4,597	−42	1,191,099	299,289	1,490,388	335,703	0	1,154,685
2005	732,005	28,167	246,527	200,654	3,611	−354	1,210,610	323,749	1,534,359	359,626	1,183	1,175,916
2006	746,030	29,944	252,359	216,667	3,758	66	1,248,825	361,541	1,610,366	401,614	592	1,209,344
2001 Q1	161,204	6,873	53,609	44,158	1,675	−26	267,565	71,295	339,027	73,841	0	265,267
2001 Q2	162,333	6,788	53,894	44,888	1,793	202	270,071	69,333	339,452	73,937	0	265,573
2001 Q3	164,239	6,762	54,600	45,017	1,726	30	272,481	67,921	340,353	73,327	0	267,163
2001 Q4	165,550	6,732	55,256	44,140	383	136	272,216	69,145	341,373	73,344	0	268,214
2002 Q1	167,588	6,762	55,756	44,562	1,059	66	275,814	69,440	345,256	75,709	0	269,595
2002 Q2	168,803	6,756	56,288	45,610	409	48	277,926	71,533	349,504	78,367	0	271,044
2002 Q3	169,715	6,793	56,429	46,422	520	62	280,004	71,056	351,089	78,006	0	273,034
2002 Q4	170,727	6,819	56,395	48,107	301	7	282,495	68,564	351,013	76,624	0	274,435
2003 Q1	171,828	6,843	57,099	46,805	−477	−8	282,249	72,662	354,921	78,836	0	276,082
2003 Q2	174,146	6,779	57,684	46,131	−635	94	284,342	70,610	354,945	77,283	0	277,686
2003 Q3	175,140	6,790	58,445	45,964	2,223	−68	288,498	70,334	358,825	78,089	0	280,743
2003 Q4	176,046	6,773	59,471	47,800	2,872	−55	292,601	71,791	364,396	80,634	0	283,734
2004 Q1	178,197	6,830	59,969	49,353	−439	112	294,023	73,389	367,412	81,648	0	285,764
2004 Q2	180,362	6,805	59,530	49,159	1,042	−90	296,808	74,861	371,670	83,313	0	288,357
2004 Q3	181,032	6,826	60,002	49,832	1,047	−96	298,644	75,097	373,741	84,300	0	289,441
2004 Q4	181,843	6,866	60,628	49,311	2,947	32	301,624	75,942	377,565	86,442	0	291,123
2005 Q1	182,466	7,005	60,858	49,393	1,894	−158	301,458	75,952	377,410	85,898	253	291,764
2005 Q2	182,306	6,987	61,613	49,334	797	86	301,122	79,576	380,698	87,920	300	293,078
2005 Q3	183,174	7,042	61,885	50,642	853	−201	303,394	82,357	385,751	91,483	320	294,588
2005 Q4	184,059	7,133	62,171	51,285	67	−81	304,636	85,864	390,500	94,325	310	296,486
2006 Q1	184,321	7,340	63,014	52,274	703	−128	307,523	95,198	402,721	104,029	181	298,873
2006 Q2	186,226	7,430	62,884	53,473	2,680	233	312,925	96,228	409,153	108,003	153	301,303
2006 Q3	186,733	7,523	63,087	54,606	1,258	−29	313,178	85,206	398,384	95,152	134	303,366
2006 Q4	188,750	7,651	63,374	56,314	−883	−10	315,199	84,909	400,108	94,430	124	305,802
2007 Q1	189,632	7,694	63,712	56,937	−699	73	317,347	84,201	401,548	93,809	151	307,890

Percentage change, quarter on corresponding quarter of previous year

	Households	Non-profit institutions	General government	Gross fixed capital formation			Total	Exports of goods and services	Gross final expenditure	less imports of goods and services		Gross domestic at product market prices
2001 Q1	2.1	3.9	1.8	3.0			2.8	9.7	4.3	9.0		2.9
2001 Q2	2.9	0.6	1.6	5.5			3.2	3.0	3.1	6.1		2.3
2001 Q3	3.4	−1.6	2.8	3.7			3.0	1.0	2.6	3.6		2.3
2001 Q4	4.0	−3.0	3.3	−1.6			2.7	−1.6	1.7	0.7		2.1
2002 Q1	4.0	−1.6	4.0	0.9			3.1	−2.6	1.8	2.5		1.6
2002 Q2	4.0	−0.5	4.4	1.6			2.9	3.2	3.0	6.0		2.1
2002 Q3	3.3	0.5	3.3	3.1			2.8	4.6	3.2	6.4		2.2
2002 Q4	3.1	1.3	2.1	9.0			3.8	−0.8	2.8	4.5		2.3
2003 Q1	2.5	1.2	2.4	5.0			2.3	4.6	2.8	4.1		2.4
2003 Q2	3.2	0.3	2.5	1.1			2.3	−1.3	1.6	−1.4		2.5
2003 Q3	3.2	0.0	3.6	−1.0			3.0	−1.0	2.2	0.1		2.8
2003 Q4	3.1	−0.7	5.5	−0.6			3.6	4.7	3.8	5.2		3.4
2004 Q1	3.7	−0.2	5.0	5.4			4.2	1.0	3.5	3.6		3.5
2004 Q2	3.6	0.4	3.2	6.6			4.4	6.0	4.7	7.8		3.8
2004 Q3	3.4	0.5	2.7	8.4			3.5	6.8	4.2	8.0		3.1
2004 Q4	3.3	1.4	1.9	3.2			3.1	5.8	3.6	7.2		2.6
2005 Q1	2.4	2.6	1.5	0.1			2.5	3.5	2.7	5.2		2.1
2005 Q2	1.1	2.7	3.5	0.4			1.5	6.3	2.4	5.5		1.6
2005 Q3	1.2	3.2	3.1	1.6			1.6	9.7	3.2	8.5		1.8
2005 Q4	1.2	3.9	2.5	4.0			1.0	13.1	3.4	9.1		1.8
2006 Q1	1.0	4.8	3.5	5.8			2.0	25.3	6.7	21.1		2.4
2006 Q2	2.2	6.3	2.1	8.4			3.9	20.9	7.5	22.8		2.8
2006 Q3	1.9	6.8	1.9	7.8			3.2	3.5	3.3	4.0		3.0
2006 Q4	2.5	7.3	1.9	9.8			3.5	−1.1	2.5	0.1		3.1
2007 Q1	2.9	4.8	1.1	8.9			3.2	−11.6	−0.3	−9.8		3.0

Notes:

1 Non-profit institutions serving households (NPISH).
2 This series includes a quarterly alignment adjustment.

Source: Office for National Statistics

Labour market summary

Last updated: 13/06/07

United Kingdom (thousands), seasonally adjusted

	All	Total economically active	Total in employment	Unemployed	Economically inactive	Economic activity rate (%)	Employment rate (%)	Unemployment rate (%)	Economic inactivity rate (%)
					All aged 16 and over				
	1	2	3	4	5	6	7	8	9
All persons	MGSL	MGSF	MGRZ	MGSC	MGSI	MGWG	MGSR	MGSX	YBTC
Feb-Apr 2005	47,684	30,060	28,649	1,411	17,625	63.0	60.1	4.7	37.0
Feb-Apr 2006	48,069	30,545	28,925	1,620	17,524	63.5	60.2	5.3	36.5
May-Jul 2006	48,162	30,666	28,964	1,702	17,496	63.7	60.1	5.5	36.3
Aug-Oct 2006	48,254	30,700	29,005	1,695	17,555	63.6	60.1	5.5	36.4
Nov-Jan 2007	48,347	30,715	29,022	1,692	17,633	63.5	60.0	5.5	36.5
Feb-Apr 2007	48,440	30,689	29,012	1,677	17,751	63.4	59.9	5.5	36.6
Male	MGSM	MGSG	MGSA	MGSD	MGSJ	MGWH	MGSS	MGSY	YBTD
Feb-Apr 2005	23,108	16,303	15,473	830	6,805	70.6	67.0	5.1	29.4
Feb-Apr 2006	23,319	16,535	15,589	945	6,785	70.9	66.9	5.7	29.1
May-Jul 2006	23,370	16,585	15,602	983	6,785	71.0	66.8	5.9	29.0
Aug-Oct 2006	23,422	16,631	15,652	979	6,791	71.0	66.8	5.9	29.0
Nov-Jan 2007	23,474	16,635	15,668	967	6,840	70.9	66.7	5.8	29.1
Feb-Apr 2007	23,527	16,651	15,684	967	6,876	70.8	66.7	5.8	29.2
Female	MGSN	MGSH	MGSB	MGSE	MGSK	MGWI	MGST	MGSZ	YBTE
Feb-Apr 2005	24,576	13,756	13,176	581	10,820	56.0	53.6	4.2	44.0
Feb-Apr 2006	24,750	14,010	13,336	674	10,740	56.6	53.9	4.8	43.4
May-Jul 2006	24,792	14,081	13,362	719	10,711	56.8	53.9	5.1	43.2
Aug-Oct 2006	24,833	14,068	13,352	716	10,764	56.7	53.8	5.1	43.3
Nov-Jan 2007	24,873	14,080	13,354	726	10,793	56.6	53.7	5.2	43.4
Feb-Apr 2007	24,913	14,038	13,328	711	10,875	56.3	53.5	5.1	43.7

	All	Total economically active	Total in employment	Unemployed	Economically inactive	Economic activity rate (%)	Employment rate (%)	Unemployment rate (%)	Economic inactivity rate (%)
					All aged 16 to 59/64				
	10	11	12	13	14	15	16	17	18
All persons	YBTF	YBSK	YBSE	YBSH	YBSN	MGSO	MGSU	YBTI	YBTL
Feb-Apr 2005	36,933	28,995	27,603	1,392	7,938	78.5	74.7	4.8	21.5
Feb-Apr 2006	37,208	29,375	27,782	1,593	7,834	78.9	74.7	5.4	21.1
May-Jul 2006	37,274	29,477	27,804	1,674	7,797	79.1	74.6	5.7	20.9
Aug-Oct 2006	37,323	29,488	27,820	1,668	7,835	79.0	74.5	5.7	21.0
Nov-Jan 2007	37,364	29,487	27,817	1,670	7,877	78.9	74.4	5.7	21.1
Feb-Apr 2007	37,405	29,451	27,799	1,652	7,954	78.7	74.3	5.6	21.3
Male	YBTG	YBSL	YBSF	YBSI	YBSO	MGSP	MGSV	YBTJ	YBTM
Feb-Apr 2005	19,096	15,936	15,116	821	3,160	83.5	79.2	5.1	16.5
Feb-Apr 2006	19,266	16,138	15,203	935	3,128	83.8	78.9	5.8	16.2
May-Jul 2006	19,308	16,187	15,216	971	3,121	83.8	78.8	6.0	16.2
Aug-Oct 2006	19,347	16,221	15,253	968	3,126	83.8	78.8	6.0	16.2
Nov-Jan 2007	19,385	16,225	15,266	959	3,160	83.7	78.8	5.9	16.3
Feb-Apr 2007	19,423	16,238	15,283	955	3,185	83.6	78.7	5.9	16.4
Female	YBTH	YBSM	YBSG	YBSJ	YBSP	MGSQ	MGSW	YBTK	YBTN
Feb-Apr 2005	17,837	13,059	12,487	571	4,778	73.2	70.0	4.4	26.8
Feb-Apr 2006	17,942	13,237	12,579	657	4,706	73.8	70.1	5.0	26.2
May-Jul 2006	17,966	13,290	12,587	703	4,676	74.0	70.1	5.3	26.0
Aug-Oct 2006	17,976	13,267	12,567	701	4,709	73.8	69.9	5.3	26.2
Nov-Jan 2007	17,979	13,262	12,551	711	4,717	73.8	69.8	5.4	26.2
Feb-Apr 2007	17,982	13,213	12,516	697	4,769	73.5	69.6	5.3	26.5

Notes:

Relationship between columns: 1 = 2 + 5; 2 = 3 + 4; 6 = 2/1; 7 = 3/1; 8 = 4/2;
9 = 5/1; 10 = 11 + 14; 11 = 12 + 13; 15 = 11/10; 16 = 12/10; 17 = 13/11; 18 = 14/10
The Labour Force Survey is a survey of the population of private households, student halls of residence
and NHS accommodation.

Source: Labour Force Survey, Office for National Statistics
Labour Market Statistics Helpline: 020 7533 6094

Prices

Last updated: 12/06/07

Percentage change over 12 months

	Consumer prices						Producer prices (Not seasonally adjusted, except for series PLLW, RNPE and RNPF)			
	Consumer prices index (CPI)			Retail prices index (RPI)			Output prices		Input prices	
	All items	CPI excluding indirect taxes (CPIY)[1]	CPI at constant tax rates (CPI-CT)	All items	All items excluding mortgage interest payments (RPIX)	All items excluding mortgage interest payments and indirect taxes (RPIY)[2]	All manufactured products	Excluding food, beverages, tobacco and petroleum products	Materials and fuels purchased by manufacturing industry	Excluding food, beverages, tobacco and petroleum products
	D7G7	EL2S	EAD6	CZBH	CDKQ	CBZX	PLLU[3]	PLLW[3]	RNPE[3]	RNPF[3]
2003 Jan	1.3			2.9	2.7	2.9	1.3	0.9	1.7	−2.2
2003 Feb	1.6			3.2	3.0	3.1	1.5	1.1	2.5	−2.0
2003 Mar	1.5			3.1	3.0	3.2	2.1	1.3	0.8	−1.5
2003 Apr	1.4			3.1	3.0	2.9	1.6	1.3	−1.3	−0.6
2003 May	1.3			3.0	2.9	2.7	1.1	1.2	−0.1	−0.2
2003 Jun	1.1			2.9	2.8	2.7	1.1	1.2	0.0	−1.2
2003 Jul	1.3			3.1	2.9	2.8	1.3	1.3	0.6	−0.5
2003 Aug	1.4			2.9	2.9	2.7	1.5	1.2	1.9	0.0
2003 Sep	1.4			2.8	2.8	2.7	1.4	1.4	1.3	1.0
2003 Oct	1.4			2.6	2.7	2.4	1.5	1.3	2.5	1.2
2003 Nov	1.3			2.5	2.5	2.1	1.7	1.4	4.6	1.7
2003 Dec	1.3	1.1	1.1	2.8	2.6	2.2	1.8	1.5	2.0	0.4
2004 Jan	1.4	1.5	1.3	2.6	2.4	2.0	1.6	1.4	−0.3	0.0
2004 Feb	1.3	1.3	1.1	2.5	2.3	1.9	1.6	1.5	−1.3	−0.5
2004 Mar	1.1	1.1	1.0	2.6	2.1	1.7	1.4	1.5	0.9	−0.1
2004 Apr	1.1	1.1	1.0	2.5	2.0	1.8	1.8	1.3	2.9	−0.2
2004 May	1.5	1.4	1.3	2.8	2.3	2.2	2.5	1.4	5.6	0.7
2004 Jun	1.6	1.5	1.4	3.0	2.3	2.3	2.6	1.4	3.7	1.3
2004 Jul	1.4	1.4	1.2	3.0	2.2	2.0	2.6	1.7	3.7	1.4
2004 Aug	1.3	1.3	1.1	3.2	2.2	2.0	2.8	2.2	4.6	2.3
2004 Sep	1.1	1.0	0.9	3.1	1.9	1.7	3.1	2.3	8.1	3.8
2004 Oct	1.2	1.2	1.1	3.3	2.1	2.0	3.5	2.9	9.2	4.8
2004 Nov	1.5	1.4	1.4	3.4	2.2	2.2	3.5	2.9	6.7	4.6
2004 Dec	1.7	1.7	1.6	3.5	2.5	2.5	2.9	2.5	4.4	4.2
2005 Jan	1.6	1.7	1.5	3.2	2.1	2.0	2.6	2.5	9.6	7.5
2005 Feb	1.7	1.7	1.6	3.2	2.1	2.0	2.7	2.5	11.0	8.2
2005 Mar	1.9	2.0	1.8	3.2	2.4	2.3	2.9	2.4	11.1	7.4
2005 Apr	1.9	2.0	1.9	3.2	2.3	2.3	3.3	2.6	10.0	7.0
2005 May	1.9	2.0	1.8	2.9	2.1	2.2	2.7	2.5	7.6	6.5
2005 Jun	2.0	2.2	1.9	2.9	2.2	2.2	2.5	2.3	12.0	7.4
2005 Jul	2.3	2.5	2.3	2.9	2.4	2.5	3.1	2.2	13.9	8.6
2005 Aug	2.4	2.6	2.3	2.8	2.3	2.3	3.0	1.9	12.8	7.5
2005 Sep	2.5	2.6	2.4	2.7	2.5	2.5	3.3	2.1	10.5	5.7
2005 Oct	2.3	2.5	2.3	2.5	2.4	2.3	2.6	1.4	8.9	7.0
2005 Nov	2.1	2.3	2.1	2.4	2.3	2.3	2.3	1.3	13.6	9.6
2005 Dec	1.9	2.1	1.8	2.2	2.0	2.0	2.4	1.7	17.9	12.1
2006 Jan	1.9	2.1	1.9	2.4	2.3	2.3	2.9	1.8	15.8	10.3
2006 Feb	2.0	2.1	2.0	2.4	2.3	2.3	2.9	1.8	15.4	10.7
2006 Mar	1.8	1.9	1.7	2.4	2.1	2.2	2.5	1.9	12.9	10.1
2006 Apr	2.0	2.1	2.0	2.6	2.4	2.3	2.5	2.2	15.2	10.1
2006 May	2.2	2.3	2.2	3.0	2.9	2.8	3.1	2.4	13.5	8.9
2006 Jun	2.5	2.6	2.4	3.3	3.1	3.2	3.4	2.9	11.1	8.7
2006 Jul	2.4	2.4	2.3	3.3	3.1	3.2	2.9	2.5	10.5	8.2
2006 Aug	2.5	2.6	2.4	3.4	3.3	3.4	2.7	2.3	8.0	7.8
2006 Sep	2.4	2.6	2.3	3.6	3.2	3.3	1.9	2.1	5.1	7.0
2006 Oct	2.4	2.7	2.3	3.7	3.2	3.3	1.6	2.6	4.7	6.1
2006 Nov	2.7	3.0	2.6	3.9	3.4	3.6	1.8	2.6	3.3	4.7
2006 Dec	3.0	3.2	2.9	4.4	3.8	3.9	2.2	2.5	2.1	2.8
2007 Jan	2.7	2.9	2.6	4.2	3.5	3.7	2.2	2.5	−2.1	1.7
2007 Feb	2.8	2.9	2.6	4.6	3.7	3.9	2.3	2.6	−0.8	1.4
2007 Mar	3.1	3.1	2.9	4.8	3.9	4.0	2.7	2.7	0.7	2.4
2007 Apr	2.8	2.9	2.6	4.5	3.6	3.7	2.5	2.4	−0.7	2.2
2007 May	2.5	2.6	2.3	4.3	3.3	3.4	2.5	2.3	1.1	3.4

Notes: Source: Office for National Statistics

1 The taxes excluded are VAT, duties, insurance premium tax, air passenger duty and stamp duty on share transactions.
2 The taxes excluded are council tax, VAT, duties, vehicle excise duty, insurance premium tax and air passenger duty.
3 Derived from these identification (CDID) codes.

NOTES TO TABLES

Identification (CDID) codes

The four-character identification code at the top of each alpha column of data is the ONS reference for that series of data on our time series database. Please quote the relevant code if you contact us about the data.

Conventions

Where figures have been rounded to the final digit, there may be an apparent slight discrepancy between the sum of the constituent items and the total shown. Although figures may be given in unrounded form to facilitate readers' calculation of percentage changes, rates of change, etc, this does not imply that the figures can be estimated to this degree of precision as they may be affected by sampling variability or imprecision in estimation methods.

The following standard symbols are used:

- ..   not available
- -   nil or negligible
- P   provisional
- –   break in series
- R   revised
- r   series revised from indicated entry onwards

CONCEPTS AND DEFINITIONS

Labour Force Survey 'monthly' estimates

Labour Force Survey (LFS) results are three-monthly averages, so consecutive months' results overlap. Comparing estimates for overlapping three-month periods can produce more volatile results, which can be difficult to interpret.

Labour market summary

Economically active

People aged 16 and over who are either in employment or unemployed.

Economically inactive

People who are neither in employment nor unemployed. This includes those who want a job but have not been seeking work in the last four weeks, those who want a job and are seeking work but not available to start work, and those who do not want a job.

Employment and jobs

There are two ways of looking at employment: the number of people with jobs, or the number of jobs. The two concepts are not the same as one person can have more than one job. The number of people with jobs is measured by the Labour Force Survey (LFS) and includes people aged 16 or over who do paid work (as an employee or self-employed), those who have a job that they are temporarily away from, those on government-supported training and employment programmes, and those doing unpaid family work. The number of jobs is measured by workforce jobs and is the sum of employee jobs (as measured by surveys of employers), self-employment jobs from the LFS, people in HM Forces, and government-supported trainees. Vacant jobs are not included.

Unemployment

The number of unemployed people in the UK is measured through the Labour Force Survey following the internationally agreed definition recommended by the ILO (International Labour Organisation) – an agency of the United Nations.

Unemployed people:
- are without a job, want a job, have actively sought work in the last four weeks and are available to start work in the next two weeks, or
- are out of work, have found a job and are waiting to start it in the next two weeks

Other key indicators

Claimant count

The number of people claiming Jobseeker's Allowance benefits.

Earnings

A measure of the money people receive in return for work done, gross of tax. It includes salaries and, unless otherwise stated, bonuses but not unearned income, benefits in kind or arrears of pay.

Productivity

Whole economy output per worker is the ratio of Gross Value Added (GVA) at basic prices and Labour Force Survey (LFS) total employment. Manufacturing output per filled job is the ratio of manufacturing output (from the Index of Production) and productivity jobs for manufacturing (constrained to LFS jobs at the whole economy level).

Redundancies

The number of people who:

- were not in employment during the reference week, and
- reported that they had been made redundant in the month of, or the two calendar months prior to, the reference week

plus the number of people who:

- were in employment during the reference week, and
- started their job in the same calendar month as, or the two calendar months prior to, the reference week, and
- reported that they had been made redundant in the month of, or the two calendar months prior to, the reference week

Unit wage costs

A measure of the cost of wages and salaries per unit of output.

Vacancies

The statistics are based on ONS's Vacancy Survey of businesses. The survey is designed to provide comprehensive estimates of the stock of vacancies across the economy, excluding those in agriculture, forestry and fishing. Vacancies are defined as positions for which employers are actively seeking recruits from outside their business or organisation. More information on labour market concepts, sources and methods is available in the *Guide to Labour Market Statistics* at www.statistics.gov.uk/about/data/guides/LabourMarket/default.asp

Directory of online tables

The tables listed below are available as Excel spreadsheets via weblinks accessible from the main *Economic & Labour Market Review* (ELMR) page of the National Statistics website. Tables in sections 1, 3, 4 and 5 replace equivalent ones formerly published in *Economic Trends*, although there are one or two new tables here; others have been expanded to include, as appropriate, both unadjusted/seasonally adjusted, and current price/chained volume measure variants. Tables in sections 2 and 6 were formerly in *Labour Market Trends*. The opportunity has also been taken to extend the range of dates shown in many cases, as the online tables are not constrained by page size.

In the online tables, the four-character identification codes at the top of each data column correspond to the ONS reference for that series on our time series database. The latest data sets for the old *Economic Trends* tables and the Labour Market Statistics First Release tables are still available on this database via the 'Time Series Data' link on the National Statistics main web page. These data sets can also be accessed from links at the bottom of each section's table listings via the 'Data tables' link in the individual ELMR edition pages on the website.

Weblink: www.statistics.gov.uk/elmr_tables

Title	Frequency of update	Updated since last month
UK economic accounts		
1.01 National accounts aggregates	M	✔
1.02 Gross domestic product and gross national income	M	✔
1.03 Gross domestic product, by category of expenditure	M	✔
1.04 Gross domestic product, by category of income	M	✔
1.05 Gross domestic product and shares of income and expenditure	M	✔
1.06 Income, product and spending per head	Q	✔
1.07 Households' disposable income and consumption	M	✔
1.08 Household final consumption expenditure	M	✔
1.09 Gross fixed capital formation	M	✔
1.10 Gross value added, by category of output	M	✔
1.11 Gross value added, by category of output: service industries	M	✔
1.12 Summary capital accounts and net lending/net borrowing	Q	✔
1.13 Private non-financial corporations: allocation of primary income account	Q	✔
1.14 Private non-financial corporations: secondary distribution of income account and capital account	Q	✔
1.15 Balance of payments: current account	M	✔
1.16 Trade in goods (on a balance of payments basis)	M	✔
1.17 Measures of variability of selected economic series	Q	•
1.18 Index of services (NEW)	M	✔
Selected labour market statistics		
2.01 Summary of Labour Force Survey data	M	✔
2.02 Employment by age	M	✔
2.03 Full-time, part-time and temporary workers	M	✔
2.04 Public and private sector employment	Q	✔
2.05 Workforce jobs	Q	✔
2.06 Workforce jobs by industry	Q	✔
2.07 Actual weekly hours of work	M	✔
2.08 Usual weekly hours of work	M	✔
2.09 Unemployment by age and duration	M	✔
2.10 Claimant count levels and rates	M	✔
2.11 Claimant count by age and duration	M	✔
2.12 Economic activity by age	M	✔
2.13 Economic inactivity by age	M	✔
2.14 Economic inactivity: reasons	M	✔
2.15 Educational status, economic activity and inactivity of young people	M	✔
2.16 Average earnings – including bonuses	M	✔
2.17 Average earnings – excluding bonuses	M	✔
2.18 Productivity and unit wage costs	M	✔
2.19 Regional labour market summary	M	✔

Weblink: www.statistics.gov.uk/elmr_tables

2.20	International comparisons	M	✔
2.21	Labour disputes	M	✔
2.22	Vacancies	M	✔
2.23	Vacancies by industry	M	✔
2.24	Redundancies: levels and rates	M	✔
2.25	Redundancies: by industry	Q	•
2.26	Sampling variability for headline labour market statistics	M	✔

Prices

3.01	Producer and consumer prices	M	✔
3.02	Harmonised Indices of Consumer Prices: EU comparisons	M	✔

Selected output and demand indicators

4.01	Output of the production industries	M	✔
4.02	Engineering and construction: output and orders	M	✔
4.03	Motor vehicle and steel production	M	✔
4.04	Indicators of fixed investment in dwellings	M	✔
4.05	Number of property transactions	M	✔
4.06	Change in inventories	Q	✔
4.07	Inventory ratios	Q	•
4.08	Retail sales, new registrations of cars and credit business	M	✔
4.09	Inland energy consumption: primary fuel input basis	M	✔

Selected financial statistics

5.01	Sterling exchange rates and UK reserves	M	✔
5.02	Monetary aggregates	M	✔
5.03	Counterparts to changes in money stock M4	M	✔
5.04	Public sector receipts and expenditure	Q	✔
5.05	Public sector key fiscal indicators	M	✔
5.06	Consumer credit and other household sector borrowing	M	✔
5.07	Analysis of bank lending to UK residents	M	✔
5.08	Interest rates and yields	M	✔
5.09	A selection of asset prices	M	✔

Further labour market statistics

6.01	Working-age households	A	•
6.02	Local labour market indicators by unitary and local authority	Q	•
6.03	Employment by occupation	Q	•
6.04	Employee jobs by industry	M	✔
6.05	Employee jobs by industry division, class or group	Q	✔
6.06	Employee jobs by region and industry	Q	✔
6.07	Key productivity measures by industry	Q	✔
6.08	Total workforce hours worked per week	Q	•
6.09	Total workforce hours worked per week by region and industry group	Q	•
6.10	Job-related training received by employees	Q	•
6.11	Unemployment rates by previous occupation	Q	•

Weblink: www.statistics.gov.uk/elmr_tables

6.12	Average Earnings Index by industry: excluding and including bonuses	M	✔
6.13	Average Earnings Index: effect of bonus payments by main industrial sector	M	✔
6.14	Median earnings and hours by main industrial sector	A	•
6.15	Median earnings and hours by industry section	A	•
6.16	Index of wages per head: international comparisons	M	✔
6.17	Regional Jobseeker's Allowance claimant count rates	M	✔
6.18	Claimant count area statistics: counties, unitary and local authorities	M	✔
6.19	Claimant count area statistics: UK parliamentary constituencies	M	✔
6.20	Claimant count area statistics: constituencies of the Scottish Parliament	M	✔
6.21	Jobseeker's Allowance claimant count flows	M	✔
6.22	Number of previous Jobseeker's Allowance claims	Q	•
6.23	Interval between Jobseeker's Allowance claims	Q	•
6.24	Average duration of Jobseeker's Allowance claims by age	Q	✔
6.25	Vacancies by size of enterprise	M	✔
6.26	Redundancies: re-employment rates	Q	•
6.27	Redundancies by Government Office Region	Q	•
6.28	Redundancy rates by industry	Q	•
6.29	Labour disputes: summary	M	✔
6.30	Labour disputes: stoppages in progress	M	✔

Notes

A Annually
Q Quarterly
M Monthly

More information

Time series are available from www.statistics.gov.uk/statbase/tsdintro.asp
Subnational labour market data are available from www.statistics.gov.uk/statbase/Product.asp?vlnk=14160 and www.nomisweb.co.uk
Labour Force Survey tables are available from www.statistics.gov.uk/statbase/Product.asp?vlnk=14365
Annual Survey of Hours and Earnings data are available from www.statistics.gov.uk/StatBase/Product.asp?vlnk=13101

Contact points

Recorded announcement of latest RPI
020 7533 5866
rpi@ons.gsi.gov.uk

Labour Market Statistics Helpline
020 7533 6094
labour.market@ons.gsi.gov.uk

Earnings Customer Helpline
01633 819024
earnings@ons.gsi.gov.uk

National Statistics Customer Contact Centre
0845 601 3034
info@statistics.gsi.gov.uk

Skills and Education Network
024 7682 3439
senet@lsc.gov.uk

DfES Public Enquiry Unit
0870 000 2288

For statistical information on

Average Earnings Index (monthly)
01633 819024

Claimant count
020 7533 6094

Consumer Prices Index
020 7533 5874

Earnings
Annual Survey of Hours and Earnings
01633 819024

Basic wage rates and hours for manual workers with a collective agreement
01633 819008

Low-paid workers
01633 819024
lowpay@ons.gsi.gov.uk

Labour Force Survey
020 7533 6094
labour.market@ons.gsi.gov.uk

Economic activity and inactivity
020 7533 6094

Employment
Labour Force Survey
020 7533 6094
labour.market@ons.gsi.gov.uk

Employee jobs by industry
01633 812318

Total workforce hours worked per week
01633 812766
productivity@ons.gsi.gov.uk

**Workforce jobs series –
short-term estimates**
01633 812318
workforce.jobs@ons.gsi.gov.uk

Labour costs
01633 819024

Labour disputes
01633 819205

Labour Force Survey
020 7533 6094
labour.market@ons.gsi.gov.uk

Labour Force Survey Data Service
01633 655732
lfs.dataservice@ons.gsi.gov.uk

New Deal
0114 209 8228

Productivity and unit wage costs
01633 812766

Public sector employment
General enquiries
020 7533 6178

Source and methodology enquiries
01633 812362

Qualifications (DfES)
0870 000 2288

Redundancy statistics
020 7533 6094

Retail Prices Index
020 7533 5874
rpi@ons.gsi.gov.uk

Skills (DfES)
0114 259 4407
Skill needs surveys and research into skill shortages
0114 259 4407

Small firms (DTI)
Small Business Service (SBS)
0114 279 4439

Subregional estimates
01633 812038

Annual employment statistics
annual.employment.figures@ons.gsi.gov.uk

Annual Population Survey, local area statistics
020 7533 6130

LFS Subnational Data Service
020 7533 6135
snds@ons.gsi.gov.uk

Trade unions (DTI)
Employment relations
020 7215 5934

Training
Adult learning – work-based training (DWP)
0114 209 8236

Employer-provided training (DfES)
0114 259 4407

Travel-to-Work Areas
Composition and review
020 7533 6114

Unemployment
020 7533 6094

Vacancies
Vacancy Survey:
total stocks of vacancies
020 7533 6162

ONS economic and labour market publications

ANNUAL

Financial Statistics Explanatory Handbook

2007 edition. Palgrave Macmillan, ISBN 1-4039-9783-7. Price £45.

www.statistics.gov.uk/products/p4861.asp

Foreign Direct Investment (MA4)

2005 edition

www.statistics.gov.uk/products/p9614.asp

Input-Output analyses for the United Kingdom

2006 edition

www.statistics.gov.uk/products/p7640.asp

Research and development in UK businesses (MA14)

2005 edition

www.statistics.gov.uk/statbase/product.asp?vlnk=165

Share Ownership

2004 edition

www.statistics.gov.uk/products/p930.asp

United Kingdom Balance of Payments (Pink Book)

2006 edition. Palgrave Macmillan, ISBN 1-4039-9387-4. Price £45.

www.statistics.gov.uk/products/p1140.asp

(2007 edition available online on 20 July)

United Kingdom National Accounts (Blue Book)

2006 edition. Palgrave Macmillan, ISBN 1-4039-9388-2. Price £45.

www.statistics.gov.uk/products/p1143.asp

(2007 edition available online on 20 July)

First releases

- Annual survey of hours and earnings
- Business enterprise research and development
- Foreign direct investment
- Gross domestic expenditure on research and development
- Low pay estimates
- Regional gross value added
- Share ownership
- UK trade in services
- Work and worklessness among households

QUARTERLY

Consumer Trends

2007 quarter 1

www.statistics.gov.uk/products/p242.asp

United Kingdom Economic Accounts

2007 quarter 1. Palgrave Macmillan, ISBN 978-0-230-52618-1. Price £32.

www.statistics.gov.uk/products/p1904.asp

UK trade in goods analysed in terms of industry (MQ10)

2007 quarter 1

www.statistics.gov.uk/products/p731.asp

First releases

- Business investment
- Government deficit and debt under the Maastricht Treaty (six-monthly)
- GDP preliminary estimate
- International comparisons of productivity (six-monthly)
- Internet connectivity
- Investment by insurance companies, pension funds and trusts
- Productivity
- Profitability of UK companies
- Public sector employment
- UK Balance of Payments
- UK National Accounts
- UK output, income and expenditure

MONTHLY

Financial Statistics

June 2007. Palgrave Macmillan, ISBN 978-0-230-52589-4. Price £45.

www.statistics.gov.uk/products/p376.asp

Focus on Consumer Price Indices

May 2007

www.statistics.gov.uk/products/p867.asp

Monthly review of external trade statistics (MM24)

May 2007

www.statistics.gov.uk/products/p613.asp

Producer Price Indices (MM22)

May 2007

www.statistics.gov.uk/products/p2208.asp

First releases

- Consumer price Indices
- Index of distribution
- Index of production
- Labour market statistics
- Labour market statistics: regional
- Producer prices
- Public sector finances
- Retail sales index
- UK trade

OTHER

The ONS Productivity Handbook: a statistical overview and guide

Palgrave Macmillan, ISBN 978-0-230-57301-7. Price £55.

www.statistics.gov.uk/about/data/guides/productivity/default.asp

Labour Market Review

2006 edition. Palgrave Macmillan, ISBN 1-4039-9735-7. Price £40.

www.statistics.gov.uk/products/p4315.asp

National Accounts Concepts, Sources and Methods

www.statistics.gov.uk/products/p1144.asp

Sector classification guide (MA23)

www.statistics.gov.uk/products/p7163.asp

Recent articles

We only credit authors in the articles themselves.

Future articles

List is provisional and subject to change.